Jim Henderson

11/10/15

Was blind, but now I see

Life stories (and lessons) in my fight against Age-Related Macular Degeneration

Jim Hindman

FOUNDER OF JIFFY LUBE INTERNATIONAL

HINDSIGHT PUBLISHING

Published by:
Hindsight Publishing
2322 Nicodemus Road
Westminster, MD 21157

To purchase copies of this book,
contact the publisher at the mailing address above,
or by email at: wjamesh@aol.com.

Cover and text design: George Lois
Edited by: Carol Cartaino and Patrick Dempsey
ISBN: 978-0-692-26741-7

DEDICATION

This book would have never materialized except for two very special people who impacted the life of a little boy who scarcely knew his father and felt unwanted by his mother.

Almost from birth, my childhood could be described as nothing less than atypical, but it would be my maternal grandparents, living on a farm near Volin, South Dakota, who brought love, caring, and discipline into my life. They provided a sense of belonging, molded my character through guidance and direction, and created an attitude of never, never giving up that would impact all of the events, people, and opportunities I would encounter later in life.

My Grandma Wharton died in 1944 and Grandpa Wharton in 1954. In writing and reflecting on my life, it became apparent that their influence and example were very much a part of who I became. I will always be grateful for their love and kindness and the foundation they provided — especially my grandfather.

His work ethic, strong commitment, determination, and courage demonstrated to an impressible little boy how it was possible to succeed regardless of the challenges.

It is with sincere humility, immeasurable love, and gratitude that I dedicate my story to these two wonderful people, who shared their love, provided stability, taught me the meaning of "home," demonstrated generosity through caring for others, and set an example of integrity…all of which shaped my life ever after.

**To my maternal grandparents —
Thomas and Mary Wharton**

What though the radiance which was once so bright

Be now for ever taken from my sight,

Though nothing can bring back the hour

Of splendour in the grass, of glory in the flower;

We will grieve not, rather find

Strength in what remains behind…

William Wordsworth

TABLE OF CONTENTS

INTRODUCTION

My name is Jim Hindman, perhaps best known as the founder of Jiffy Lube International. Though I am quite an ordinary man, my life has been anything but. After many life and business adventures, I was diagnosed with early-stage age-related macular degeneration (AMD) at age fifty-seven. My battle with this disease — and the prospect of blindness — was a long and hard-fought one. It was costly, plagued by setbacks, discouragement, loss of freedoms, increased dependency, and withdrawal in business and social settings. But I was certain an answer was out there and I would find it.

You will find in these pages not only a true-life account of what it is like to be afflicted by AMD, and my search to overcome blindness, but more importantly, a story of hope and inspiration.

This has been a hard book for me to write, since my background and temperament are such that thinking about the emotional aspect of some things is difficult and troubling. But I've done my best to give you a full and honest accounting of it all.

Contrary to what it may say in the medical charts, AMD doesn't just assault a pair of eyes. It attacks a whole person — body, mind, soul, and spirit. I want you to know me as a person, so you will understand how devastating the diagnosis and prognosis were to me, and also how my life equipped me to work through the initial denial and depression, to stand up to and fight against this new enemy. I hope that by sharing my own journey I will encourage you to reflect on your own life and how the challenges you've faced have, in fact, strengthened and readied you to fight on also.

The biggest part of the story of my life with macular degeneration is the success I have experienced with the IMT™

(Implantable Miniature Telescope). Although I was initially told that there was nothing to be done for my vision loss, ultimately I never abandoned hope or stopped searching for something I *could* do. That something, after much discouragement and many false leads, came in 2012 with the IMT™. From vision of 20/400, I have improved to 20/60 in my IMT™ implanted eye. Can you imagine?! **I was literally blind, but now I can see!**

Although you will learn a great deal about the IMT™ in these pages, and hear me sing its praises often, please be assured that I have no commercial interest in this invention — only a very personal experience with it.

As I write this, it has been two years since I had the surgery. Getting used to using my telescopic eye has not been easy — it has been downright frustrating at times. This frustration is one reason for telling my story. My hope is to make this experience better for others facing it. But — and even more importantly — I want to share the entire breadth of my experience with AMD, to give you information I never had when I was diagnosed with AMD.

Throughout my career, recognizing a need and then finding a way to fill it was my main motivation and a real source of satisfaction. The challenge of age-related macular degeneration and the pursuit of a cure is not unlike the challenge in the forties and fifties when polio was attacking and crippling people all over the world — men, women, and children. Just as control of polio was eventually possible as a result of the discovery of the Salk vaccine, we must aim for the same in the 21st century with AMD. As research continues and technology advances, ever-better products, treatments, and surgical procedures are being developed and perfected to someday conquer this destroyer. Until that time, educating those who have and will face the changes and challenges this disease brings is my priority. At least eleven million Americans currently suffer from age-related macular degeneration, and this number is going to skyrocket as the population ages. The AMD experience receives little attention, and greater awareness of the disease is essential. This is the need I am trying to fill with *Was blind, but now I see.*

Modern medicine and a dedicated, talented group of physicians and specialists at Wilmer Eye Institute at Johns Hopkins Hospital have given me a new lease on life. And a very, very precious gift — the ability to see once again! It is my wish and desire to give back in some small way for this. Thus, the proceeds from the sale of this book will be given to efforts aimed at AMD and low-vision *education, rehabilitation*, and *research*. Through the Lions Clubs International Foundation (IL), the Wilmer Eye Institute at Johns Hopkins (MD), and the Wills Eye Hospital (PA), I believe the awareness and money raised by the sale of this book will go a long way in helping AMD patients now, and to ultimately eradicate this debilitating disease in the future.

There are no doubt numerous life lessons that can be gleaned from my AMD experience, but the following was paramount for me: **never, never, never give up**, no matter what the challenge or obstacle. Yes, as the days grew darker and darker due to the progression of macular degeneration, I had to fight the feeling that regaining my vision was an insurmountable challenge. But, as they say, "Quitters never win and winners never quit!" I was a winner because I continued to have hope when all seemed hopeless. And, though I came close many times, I never gave up. I believe with all of my heart that if you decide to never give up, you can be a winner too!

A special note about this edition

Much thought went into the design of this book. While we earnestly desired to include color photos throughout, and vibrant images illustrating different aspects of AMD, the Hindman Foundation decided it more prudent to avoid the expense associated with this. After all, our goal is to raise money for AMD-related causes.

Knowing how valuable these images are to the telling of this story and to your enjoyment of it, we decided instead to create a special photo section on our website, wasblindbutnowisee.com. We invite you to visit this site, where we have added pictures of myself and my family, images relating to AMD, and short videos which tell more of my own story and the story of AMD.

One last note about design: We realize that often typeface selection is mainly a matter of personal or artistic preference. However, with the low-vision population in mind, we have chosen a simple, straight-lined font that has proven to be easier for low vision patients to read.

CHAPTER 1
UNWELCOMED

Meager Beginnings

An unplanned and unwanted pregnancy drove Dorothy-Wharton Hindman back to her parents' farm in Volin, South Dakota. There, on November 10th, 1935, at 8:04 a.m., nineteen-year-old Dorothy and sixteen-year-old Robert became the reluctant parents of Willis James Hindman — Jim.

The unwelcome pregnancy forced Dorothy and Robert into a marriage neither of them wanted or were willing to sustain. They separated frequently, finally divorcing in November of 1940, but not before having two more boys, Robert in 1938 and Harry Thomas in 1939. Even while married, my father, chasing a dream of playing semi-professional baseball, refused parental and spousal responsibility, leaving my mother to fend for herself and her three boys. It was survival on bare minimum; we always wore hand-me-down clothes and were lucky to have a bed and a meal at the end of the day.

We made the most of our one-room apartment in downtown Sioux City, Iowa. My brothers and I shared a single bed, my mother did her best to find sleep on a worn out cot. Besides a small wooden kitchen table, and three old chairs, there was no other furniture in the apartment. We did have a closet in one corner, though, a closet I came to know quite well. I served many sentences for crimes I was sure I had never committed in that closet. Lengthy terms meant both restless days and restless nights in the dark, cramped space.

Whether it was simply her natural disposition, stress over providing for her children, anger about my father's failings, or a combination of them all, my mother never hesitated to display contempt for her lot in life, or the distaste she had for us boys. Often her rage would culminate in a furious scramble through the tiny apartment. She would wield a hefty old razor strop and start swinging it like a woman gone mad, forcing me to zigzag around until I reached the bed. I'd slide under it and wrap my hands and feet around the bedsprings as she'd yank and yank on the bed. Finally she would tire and I would escape the victor.

In those years, following the crash of 1929, jobs were scarce. Although the war created many new opportunities for women, my mother was uneducated, which limited her earning potential. She made just $3,000 over a five-year period, beginning in 1941 — roughly $600 per year, which, even for that time, was far less than adequate for a family of four. When welfare assistance failed to sustain us, my mother found work cleaning houses and hotel rooms. Despite all her efforts, we struggled just to get by.

That small apartment was not our only home, though. On more than a few occasions my mother woke my brothers and me and ordered us to quickly gather as many possessions as we could carry. We then fled into the dark streets of the city to escape our rent payment. Having exhausted all possible options and with nowhere else to turn, my mother and we three boys, too overcome with stress and exhaustion to care, made our beds on the cold, hard streets of Sioux City.

Hidden Potential

My brothers and I were often without adult supervision, and the streets called out to me. Driven by my natural curiosity and fearlessness, I answered. It was on the streets of Sioux City that I got my first lessons in success and failure.

Although I did the best I could to keep my brothers safe on the streets, we had few toys or games, so entertainment often came in the form of deliberately sticking our necks out. One of our most prized pastimes was visiting the train yards, where we would hop in front of oncoming freights, only to dive out of the way at the last second.

The junk man who wandered the train yards and alleys taught me that I could pick up the coal that fell off the side of the trains, sell it, or depending on where we were living at the time, use it in our stove at home. My thoughts turned from having reckless fun to uncovering hidden potential, and I began to search for "nothings" to turn into "somethings." I wanted to prove myself. I wanted to show that I was not a mistake, that I could be something.

My Earliest Enterprises

At an early age, I became the man of the house. My mother could barely take care of herself, and my two younger brothers looked to me for their most fundamental needs. When I was six, I knew it was time to get a job and help the family. Like many youngsters of the day, I went to the streets for employment as a shoeshiner and paperboy.

After a few months of figuring things out, I secured Sergeant Bluff, a five-mile train ride south from Sioux City, as my exclusive territory. The train and the city were *my* market. My success as a paperboy kept me out on the streets, and, to my delight, out of the apartment. As an added benefit and incentive, every penny I brought in meant just a little less emotional and physical abuse back at home.

Ain't It Great!

The day World War II ended was my best day in the newspaper business. I never made it down to the Bluffs that day. I didn't need to. Crowds filled the streets. Headlines of *Peace* and *War Over* emblazoned the streamers of extra editions. The papers sold like hotcakes that day, especially in all the bars and brothels on lower 4th Street. Of course, serving this market meant entering the bars and houses of ill repute, but this was business. The brothels became a hotspot. I was ignorant of the activities in the rooms above, and the ladies were always kind and aided me in my business endeavors. They would insist their male customers purchase a paper or take me up on a shine. Plus, the entertainment provided by the ladies often led to a tip or two. "Here, kid, keep the change." I'd flick the coin into the air with my thumb and say, "Ain't it great!"

Loss and Gain

I usually double-timed my jobs, selling newspapers with my shoeshine box at the ready, looking for any opportunity to make that extra sale. One evening, while I was walking home with my shoeshine box slung over my shoulder, three older boys emerged from an alley. They walked right up to me and demanded, "Give us your money!"

Frightened, and unsure what to do, I turned over every cent in my pocket. I'd lost everything I'd earned that day. My eyes welled with tears. I collapsed under the weight of humiliation as I tried to figure out which was worse: being mugged or having to tell my mother about it. Whatever they took from me, at least those boys didn't beat me. I was sure my mother's reaction wouldn't be as considerate.

Head hung between my knees, teetering between feelings of shame and fear, I was interrupted again by a strange call. "Hey, kid, until you learn to stand up for yourself, you'll never have anything in this life."

Lifting my head as I wiped the tears from my eyes, I spotted a man leaning nonchalantly in the shadows of a nearby alley. Apparently, he had witnessed the entire incident. I wondered why he hadn't helped, why he had just stood by and watched while my money was taken from me. But, regardless, I took his words to heart.

"Yes, sir," I said as I pushed myself off the pavement and scampered home, not waiting around to see who else might be interested in conversing with me that night. I returned home poorer, though certainly wiser.

A few days later, those same three boys appeared with the same demand. But this time I was ready. Without hesitation I swung my shoeshine box with as much little-boy-strength as I could muster, striking one of the hoodlums square in the face. All three of them turned and ran, their tails tucked tightly between their legs. Amazed, I thought to myself, "It really does work!"

From then on, the wise and mysterious man who offered me that simple, but life-changing, advice received the best shoeshine possible. By not intervening, he taught me to stand up for myself, and to not let fear get the better of me. Thanks to him, it would be nearly 50 years before I was met with another challenge that I wasn't sure I had the strength to stand up to.

CHAPTER 2
MY HEROES

A Summer Retreat

The happiest days of my young life were spent on my maternal grandparents' farm in Yankton County, South Dakota. Summers provided me a much-needed respite from the turmoil of my childhood. My mother's parents, Thomas and Mary, were the two most important people in my life, and it was their love for me that kept me pointed in the right direction, despite all else that might have been going on.

I was born on that farm and so in some real way, that is where my roots are. I spent the first fifteen summers of my life there, and many other occasions, too. It was there that I built a foundation for a happy, positive outlook on life.

Farm Life with Grandpa and Grandma Wharton

In my youngest years, my experiences were mostly second-hand — just watching what everyone else was doing. Soon, I began tagging along with my grandmother, eventually helping with her chores. She managed the chickens, and it was always so exciting to see and play with all the baby chicks each spring. I got my first lesson on death when a weasel somehow made its way into the coop and killed most of the chickens. Then I got my second lesson when Grandpa hunted that weasel down to make sure nothing like that happened again! I also worked with my grandmother in the garden. Seeing something grow into a fruit or vegetable bearing plant from a little seed was just amazing.

When I got a little older I was allowed to start working with my grandfather and the other men on the farm. Up at 5:00 a.m. to milk the cows, we then spent the day in the fields, tending to one hundred and twenty acres of farmland that eventually grew to two hundred. The land produced corn, wheat, alfalfa, oats, barley, rye, grain, and more, all without the aid of tractors or modern machinery.

Meanwhile, when my grandmother had finished her farm duties, it was back into the house to clean, churn butter, can fruits and vegetables, mend the work clothes, cook the meals ... all the multiple tasks and demands of farm life. She was really the heart of the farm and the family. During my occasional winter visits, first thing in the morning she would always have all the men's boots set out in front of the wood furnace, making sure they were dry and warm before we set out to tend the farm.

Simple Pleasures

All of the work was well worth the reward at the end of the day when we enjoyed a delicious homegrown and home-cooked dinner. Then it was time to relax and enjoy the evening. We would listen to one of the early "crystal" radios, one at time of course, since it required a set of headphones. We also played a form of pool on the kitchen table, with checkers serving as our pool balls. On warm nights we'd play horseshoes. Simple times and great pleasures.

We didn't raise everything we needed on the farm, so once a week we would go to town to sell our excess cream and eggs, then go to the grocery across the street and pick up whatever else we needed with the money we had just made. We never really made a profit, but we always had just what we needed. After that, we'd usually go to Happy Jack O'Malley's, a little chicken shack, and enjoy a nice family meal out in town. In the spring, the men from the town would get together and play baseball, and it seemed everyone in town would come out to watch. I can't image how those days could have been any better.

A Mentor and Role Model

I always looked to my grandfather for guidance; he had all the answers, he was never stumped. He could do anything. His work ethic was second to none and tagging after him, watching him face all sorts of challenges with a can-do spirit taught me that I could do it, no matter what. Never before had a man taken such an interest in my life, and I was eager to hear everything he had to share, and obey every direction he so confidently dished out. He was a leader and I wanted to be just like him.

Grandpa lost all of his money in Volin State Bank after the stock market crash in 1929. To make matters worse, the region experienced a prolonged period of drought, beginning in 1932. But my grandfather knew there were few obstacles that couldn't be overcome with the sweat of one's brow and the creativity of the human mind. Grandpa Wharton bounced back stronger than ever. He managed to survive the Dust Bowl, which devastated farmers all across the plains.

An Unexpected Change

The end of each summer meant the end of my time on the farm, and a return to the city to live with my mother. When I was ten, however, my mother's struggle to provide for our family hit bottom. She'd exhausted all options. There was simply not enough to go around. Someone was looking out for us, and that someone was not happy with what they saw, so they turned my mother in. When we appeared before the judge, it was obvious the three little vagabonds standing before him needed help and direction. The judge ordered us to the Boys and Girls Home.

CHAPTER 3
A NEW HOME

Tough Love

Miss Schwant was a real disciplinarian, expertly handling the willow cane, which she reserved for the punishment of "high crimes." My punching out one of the neighborhood boys for picking on my new buddy in the Home certainly qualified. On the streets of Sioux City I learned plenty about being a fighter, mostly that opponents hate the sight of their own blood. So, a strategic punch to the nose was usually enough to win me the advantage — it was that day. The boy's mother called the Home and made sure the matrons knew I was the perpetrator. Before I even made it up the front steps Miss Schwant grabbed hold of me, dragged me into the bathroom, and began to whip my behind.

I took similar lickings before, but this time Miss Schwant meant business. Despite the welts and blood, I refused to cry. Crying was a sign of weakness, and I wasn't going to let anyone know that I was weak. So, I just took those lashes, and I took them with satisfaction. Exhausted and exasperated, Miss Schwant finally relented. Grabbing my shoulders, she turned me about-face, took me into her arms, and pleaded, "Why can't you cry?"

I didn't say a word. Dry-eyed, I looked up at Miss Schwant as tears began to roll down her cheeks.

Welcome Home

My brother Tommy and I had arrived at the Home three months earlier, while Bobby went to live with our father. A judge gave us all a choice when my father, somehow being alerted of our removal from our mother's care, unexpectedly came to stake his claim to us. Tommy, being the youngest, looked up to me as not only a brother and friend, but also as a father-type figure, so I wasn't surprised when he chose to stay with me at the Home.

 **Boys and Girls Home and Family Services**

The Boys and Girls Home of Sioux City, Iowa, began as great things often do: there was a need. There were many neglected, abused, and abandoned young children who filled the city streets and were struggling just to survive. In 1892 a Civil War widow in the city began caring for orphaned children in her home. In 1894, more women took on the mission, resulting in the formation of the Boys and Girls Home.

Three stories of red brick with towering windows, the Home stood markedly out of place in an otherwise upscale residential neighborhood. Even though I chose the Home over my father, I didn't really know what I was getting myself into. So, the first thing I did when I got to the Home was threaten to run away.

I turned to the matron in charge, Miss Schwant, and made sure she knew who she was dealing with.

"You'll never keep me here," I declared.

Apparently, I was the one who didn't know who I was dealing with. Miss Schwant was unfazed by the comment, one she had no doubt heard many times before, as she opened the door to let us in.

The first floor housed the common areas: kitchen, laundry, and library. The boys made their home on the second, with the girls on the top, third floor. The boys and girls were further segregated into three distinct living quarters, each by age. Matrons lived and stationed themselves throughout every floor. I was sure I had found myself in prison.

Much Needed Discipline

Life in the Home was much different than life in the apartment and on the streets. There was security, there was care, and there were rules. In the Home I relinquished my status of man of the house. I became part of a team. I had responsibilities and my actions had consequences. I couldn't go wherever or do whatever I pleased. For the first time, apart from time on my grandparents' farm, policies and procedures dictated my behavior.

Much like the farm, everyone had to work at the Home. The rule was, "No work, no eat!" Some kids helped in the kitchen, others in the furnace room. I was in charge of the laundry. Every morning beds were made and floors swept. A typical weekend might bring hours on our hands and knees, scrubbing floors with a brush to remove old, darkened wax, and then re-applying wax from a gallon can. Dorms, bathrooms, hallways, stairs, public areas, and offices — nothing was left untouched! The windows were washed, inside and out, twice each year, as screens were installed for the warming spring, with storm windows attached for the cooling of the fall. We learned, through practice and much sweat, the discipline and effort it took to maintain a home.

The rules and routines at the Home during this period of my life provided a feeling of security. I thrived knowing that certain things were expected of me, and that duties and assignments had to be completed at a certain time. Scheduled meals and an assigned place to sleep were just what I needed. This structure gave me the direction and purpose I needed.

On the Right Track

To hard work and disciple was added education, the real foundation of the Home. Each day I lead the other kids on the twelve block march to and from school. There we received a top-notch education, since the Home was positioned in one of the more upscale parts of Sioux City.

Religion was also an important part of our education in the Home. Saturday mornings were always devoted to Bible study. We had prayers before every meal, and engaged in all of the other rituals that go with being made to understand that you're in the hands of the Lord, and that your future is closely related to "Thy will be done." This regular religious training always included Bible school songs. Hymns such as "Jesus Loves Me, This I Know" have been part of my life ever since. This is not to say that I always followed what I learned, but I constantly returned to it.

By the time I was in junior high I knew my strengths. My time on the fields of elementary school had instilled confidence in my ability to play sports. I was fast and I was fearless. I won a wrestling championship and was runner-up in the Junior Golden Gloves competition as well as earning the Junior High American Legion Citizenship Award for "patriotism, scholarship, and service." When all of the Home mothers told me they were proud of me, I could tell I was on the right track.

Time to Go

The day I got there I wanted to run away. The day I had to leave, I wanted to stay forever.

In November of my ninth grade year I turned fifteen and so was forced to leave the comfort and security provided by the

Home. Turning fifteen meant that I had reached adulthood and was deemed capable enough to fend for myself. I suddenly found myself removed from most of the stabilizing forces in my life: my disciplined schedule, my faith in what would come tomorrow, and most importantly, my surrogate family.

I felt as if I had once again been abandoned.

By now my mother was remarried, and she half-heartedly invited me to live with her. Her husband, Marvin Cleveland, however, made it clear that I was unwelcome in "his" home.

For all intents and purposes, I was a nomad throughout my high school years, moving from one house to the next, sleeping anywhere I could, all to escape the debilitating atmosphere surrounding my mother who still refused to hide her contempt for me. "Why don't you just quit school and get a job. **You're gonna end up no good ... just like your no-good old man**."

She really believed her advice, and I was determined to prove her wrong.

CHAPTER 4
MOVING FORWARD

My Adopted Family

Prowling the streets of Sioux City looking for a place to lay my head, I practically resigned myself to yet another restless night on the hard, damp pavement. "I'll try one more," I thought to myself, making my way to the home of my good friend Carlton Tronvold. I didn't expect to see any lights on in the furrier shop, which stood just behind his home. But my heart sank when I found the house equally dark.

Desperate, I walked up the alley behind the fur shop, and went to the back of the Tronvold's house, hoping that the cellar door might be open. Luckily, it was. Cold and tired, I gave very little thought to where I might make my bed. I made my way into the warm laundry room, pulled some dirty sheets and clothes from a basket, made a nest, and fell quickly to sleep.

I'm not sure if it had been two minutes or two hours, but the next thing I knew Carlton's mom, Mayme, was standing over and staring down at me.

"What are you doing here?" she asked.

At first I was scared, and tried to think of some excuse. But, before I could even utter a word, she gently added,

"You get upstairs and get into bed."

This encounter was the defining moment of my relationship with the Tronvold family, and especially with Mayme. I came to love this woman. She was my dream mother and I knew that she loved me. To this day, it is impossible for me to find the words to pay tribute to her memory. I was always "Jimmy" to Mayme Tronvold. I was no longer just the no-good son of a no-good father. I had a family now!

Great Teachers and Coaches

With Carlton at my side, I enjoyed success throughout junior and senior high school, approaching my schoolwork, athletics, and friendships with intensity. Intensity is what got me noticed. Beginning with my American Legion Citizenship Award, I realized that my teachers and peers appreciated my efforts. I began to work harder and longer, and with greater focus. I recognized that hard work produced success.

I spent my high school years at Central High, in Sioux City, Iowa. Not only did I enjoy football and  other athletics enormously during those years, but the efforts, dedication, and commitment of a great group of teachers and coaches helped me move that next step up the ladder toward success.

Coaches Ebelheiser and Bob Lundak of the junior high football program; Mark McLarnan, Athletic Director and Head Football Coach; and Dick Young, Head Track Coach and Assistant Football Coach at Central High School, all were great coaches and unforgettable men who greatly influenced my life.

My coaches were fresh from the military. Their approach was disciplined and their programs run like a boot camp. They taught me a philosophy for life that would become a roadmap for years to come. Never give up; keep trying no matter what; it ain't over until the last whistle blows; respect your opponent, but play to win; and respect and care for your teammates and school.

People have told me, "Football is in your blood," and they

might be right. My days on the football field were glorious. The experience of running onto the field, suited up and ready to face an opponent, was absolutely thrilling. As was standing ready for kickoff, adrenaline pumping. I loved every minute of it.

Playing on the freshman football team, the camaraderie, determination, and friendship were tremendous. We won every game that year, and a few of my friends and I went on to earn our first athletic award, a school letter for our successful season. I continued my love affair with football throughout high school and earned all-city and all-state awards during my junior year. I was having a blast! Unfortunately, in my senior year a knee injury sidelined me most of the year.

I also participated in track at Central High. January ushered in the beginning of indoor practice at 6:00 a.m., which meant getting up at five, followed by walking five miles to school. Our workouts were creative obstacle courses and rope climbing, arms only, of course. When I look back, some sixty years later, I can't believe I enjoyed such strenuous conditioning.

Joining the track team was one of the best decisions I ever made in those years. Coach Young, a tough guy, fresh out of the Navy, brought out the best in his team. He inspired us, he cared, and he was fair. He achieved an unprecedented record with the team, and I believe the number of wins under Coach

Young was greater simply because we were trained better, tougher, and smarter than all the others. Coach Young planned everything down to the last detail. He coached to win, and we became winners.

Many of my lifelong habits can be credited to his influence, whether it was my dedication to out-preparing an opponent, or learning how to maximize the success of my players, students, friends, or colleagues. Coach Young taught me the value of hard work and reinforced the value of a never-say-die attitude.

Years later, at the fiftieth reunion of my high school graduating class, someone asked Coach Young who were the best athletes he had ever coached. You could have knocked me over with a feather when he included me in the group. He said I was the hardest worker he ever coached. I couldn't have been more humbled or more thrilled. A man I admired, respected, and counted as one of my heroes and mentors for many years paid me one of the greatest compliments of my lifetime.

Despite my success on the track, football was my first love, and it would ultimately become — or so I thought — my ticket out of the economic ghetto.

Football – My Ticket out of the Economic Ghetto

By January 1954 I had earned enough credits to graduate, and those formative high school years came to an end. A month before my graduation a few buddies and I joined the Marine Reserves, figuring a military career was more likely than a college career.

The Corps fit our self-image as tough guys standing tall when things got rough. The emphasis on honor, courage, and commitment, as well as the leadership training and the discipline, were all right up my alley. Reminiscent of the Boys and Girls Home, the

Marines instilled a sense of security and stability: getting up early, falling into formation, bed and barracks inspections, refinement of time management skills, and laser focus on productivity. With a fondness for the military style and no money, or any real prospects for attending college, I figured a life in the Marine Corps was going to be my destiny.

Coach Clayton Droullard, head football coach for Morningside College in Sioux City, however, had other plans for me. He had seen me play in high school, and recruited me for his team. Coach Droullard knew Central High School's season record, along with the performances of my buddies, Carlton Tronvold and Vince Arioso. Without financial assistance college was nothing but a pie-in-the-sky dream. So, when I finally met with Coach Droullard, I tried my hand at negotiation, telling him that Carlton, Vince, and I would all play for Morningside, if he could arrange something financially. He offered me a one-third tuition athletic scholarship and it was off to Morningside for the gang from Central High.

As he recounted years later, "We didn't give him any big scholarship because I didn't anticipate that he would compete — he was short, small, and not big-boned, and he would have to go up against guys fifty to seventy pounds heavier. That is pretty difficult, but I didn't rule it out, because I knew right away that the kid had a big heart." He added that this was probably the one and only time a potential recruit ever brought "bargaining chips" to the table. With my chips anted, I was ready to leave my troubled past behind.

CHAPTER 5
MORE THAN A JOCK

Only a Ditch Digger Starts at the Top

Entering Morningside in 1954 I continued to suffer from a lack of parental support, both financially and emotionally. Unlike most of my classmates, I had very few clothes or funds for necessities. While junior high and high school had shifted my focus upward, away from the poverty of my childhood and to the potential that lay ahead, the college environment, with essentially no money to my name, was a painful reminder that I was still one of the have-nots.

Even with my partial scholarship, I had to work in order to pay my tuition. The businesses in the surrounding community would contact the college and provide a list of part-time jobs, and generally the scholarship kids were given preference. Coach Droullard would call us together to announce and pass out the job opportunities. On one occasion he asked, "Can anyone milk a cow?"

I was the only guy dumb and honest enough to admit that I could. I started work as a "veterinary assistant" for Dr. Robert Tausseg, owner of the Morningside Veterinary Clinic, feeding the pets, cleaning the office, and dehorning cattle for a rousing fifty cents per head.

In addition to working for Dr. Tausseg, I waited tables at the student union and performed janitorial service at Morningside State Bank and a local church. I also cruised the parking lot of the local tavern looking for dirty cars. After finding a couple that needed a wash, I located the owners and offered to wash their car, inside and out, for two dollars. I'd drive their cars the few blocks back to campus and, using the school's cleaning supplies and hose, I'd wash the cars.

After a lot of hard work and some creative penny-pinching and stretching, I bought an old Model A — which I called *Black Beauty* — that I rented out to the frat guys. Filled with students dressed in twenties vogue, it became a regular feature of the Homecoming Parade and fraternity parties.

I took as many jobs as fit in with my class and practice schedules. Studying took place whenever and wherever it could be sandwiched in among classes, working, and my football schedule. I would get up at 5:00 a.m. to clean the bank, and be back on campus by 8:00 a.m. for my first two classes before heading to work in the cafeteria. My day continued through classes, practice, and work until late at night, when I would usually hit the books. I trained myself to need only four hours of sleep, which required that I cultivate physical, mental, and spiritual strength — not only getting bigger, faster, and stronger, but wiser, more disciplined, and smarter. Well, maybe not as smart as I could have been. After all, school came *after* work and football. But this trend couldn't be sustained.

One day Coach Droullard cornered me in the gym. He sat down beside me and challenged me, "Am I going to have to keep you in the dummy class the whole time you're here?"

He told me that he had looked at my records and knew that I could get something out of college, but only if I took it seriously. "You don't have to be a janitor all your life," Droullard said, "Why don't you try learning something while you're here?"

I accepted his challenge and went straight to hitting the books. Up to this point, college just seemed to be an opportunity to play football and get a degree. As one of my teammates said when I asked his major, "C'mon, Jim...I'm majoring in Football. Same as you!"

Before this meeting with Coach Droullard, I thought football was enough of an achievement. Considering where I came from and my precarious financial situation, I thought that my focus should be on work. When I wasn't working, football came next. But Coach made me realize I needed to apply myself to my education if I wanted to achieve real success. So, from that point forward, I made sure I attended all of my classes, participated in them, and studied more diligently. My view of college moved from an attitude of short-term tolerance to, "This is my ticket to the future."

IOU

Don Nissan was the president and owner of Morningside State Bank when I was working there as a janitor. As I cleaned, I listened to his complaints about the "skips" and bad debt accounts from month to month. During one of our discussions, he was amazed to find out I could remember the accounts and amounts with outstanding accuracy.

Eventually, Don approached me with a proposition, "How would you like to try your hand as a collection agent?" Thus the Morningside Collection Agency was born, my first government-recognized business. Don began selling me accounts for one dollar apiece, and if I successfully collected the debts, we split the proceeds fifty/fifty.

My first account was an overdue $420 note in the richest part of Sioux City. I pulled up in front of an enormous, impressive home and immediately realized there was no way that I could park my Model A in front of this nice house and still come away with the prize. So I drove around the corner, parked on a side street, and walked a block back to the house. I rang the bell and a large, hairy, cigar-smoking fellow opened the door with a growl, "What do you want?"

"I'm from the Morningside Collection Agency..." I hesitatingly replied, as he slammed the door in my face.

Now I was mad! I leaned on that doorbell until he couldn't take it any longer and finally opened the door again. Holding the notice before my face, I blurted out, "Your wife owes the Morningside State Bank $420!"

"Let me see that," he responded, pulling the paperwork from my hand. He reached into his pocket and pulled out the biggest wad of bills I'd ever seen, peeling off four hundred-dollar bills and a twenty. Then he slammed the door in my face again, and that was it. But, I was elated, I had just made $210, the most money I'd ever made at once in my life. It was great to be in business for myself!

Fringe Benefits

Around this time, in 1955, I met a cute little blonde-haired freshman named Dixie. I had also picked up another part-time job delivering prescriptions for a pharmacy. If the deliveries were close to the college, I would invite Dixie to ride along. This allowed me to kill two birds with one stone. I could work and date at the same time!

Right off the bat, Dixie and I were a team to be reckoned with. During our first year together, we got involved in the formation of the campus Independent Party, which was our response to the discovery that the fraternities barred people on the basis of race and ethnicity. After a lot of hard work and wheeling and dealing, our new party won control of student government. This small victory was only the beginning of our work together.

Another End, New Beginnings

During those college years, still serving in the Marine Reserves, I enrolled in officer training. Captain Jim Brody, a lawyer in Sioux City in his private life, was commander of our unit. Because I played football, an "angel" (an alumnus who discreetly helped players financially and otherwise) who was also a former football player and big-time lawyer in Sioux Falls approached me with a proposition before graduation — he would pay my way through law school if upon completion I would join his firm. I thought my future was set.

I shared what, to me anyway, was great news with Capt. Brody. After hearing me out, he simply replied, "You don't want to be a lawyer." I was astounded, but intrigued. Apparently he saw something different in me. Capt. Brody got in touch with his brother-in-law in Wichita, Kansas, who in turn, arranged a meeting with Otto Yankey, the head of the Hospital Administration Program at Anchor Hospital in St. Paul, Minnesota. Yankey explained the need to plan, organize, and control the systems that were part of any hospital and were only going to become more important as the healthcare system continued to expand and grow. Making sure that all of the central services — dietary, housekeeping, laundry, and all the rest — ran smoothly was critical. Hospital administration was a relatively new field at the time and Capt. Brody believed that, with my enthusiasm, drive, and determination, I would do well in it. Not knowing too much about it, I nevertheless locked right in on it, and felt that it was the thing for me.

In the spring of 1957, I graduated with honors from Morningside College with a B.A. in Business Administration. I was accepted at the University of Minnesota, and headed for Minneapolis to pursue a master's degree in Hospital Administration.

I enjoyed graduate school immensely and was lucky to have the benefit of a University of Minnesota education. Their health-care program was considered the best in the country, and the powerful and dynamic faculty impressed me. We not only had great teachers, but got to hear from lecturers, including high-level managers from the worlds of finance and government. The exposure to greatness was exhilarating and completely contagious. Among the leaders who came to the university to lecture was a man named Glen M. Reno. After his presentation, I knew I wanted to do my residency at Menorah Medical Center in Kansas City, Kansas, where Reno was Director.

Before I could begin my residency, however, I had to accomplish two things: one, convince Glen Reno to accept me as a resident in hospital administration at Menorah Medical Clinic; and, two, marry Dixie.

By this time, Dixie had also graduated from Morningside with a two-year teaching degree and was off teaching the second grade in Holstein, Iowa. The pay wasn't great, but she managed to save some money, visit me on occasion, and even helped with some of my expenses. It wasn't easy, but Dixie and I were tough, small-town kids who knew how to persevere.

I didn't know how, but I knew that if I was going to Kansas, Dixie was coming with me — as my wife! The big day finally arrived, and on June 15, 1958, Dixie and I tied the knot, thus beginning the most meaningful fifty-plus years of my life, and I hope, of

Dixie's as well. We couldn't afford an expensive wedding or honeymoon, so after the ceremony, we just packed up our few possessions and headed for Kansas City to start my residency.

CHAPTER 6
FLYING HIGH

Make or Break

Now married, fresh out of grad school, and completely broke, I was overwhelmed with a sense of urgency. Immediately upon my arrival at Menorah, I began a seven-day workweek: sixteen hours a day Monday through Friday, eight hours on Saturday, and four on Sunday. That kind of work was expected if I was to qualify for the $300 per month stipend, which we desperately needed, especially with our growing family.

On November 13, 1959, Dixie and I were blessed with the birth of a daughter, Cynthia Kay, and on March 17, 1962, our son, Timothy James. From a very young age I knew what it was like to be the man of house, but now the pressure was really on. Looking upon their precious and innocent faces, I wanted to give them the hope I never really had. Knowing that the family was relying on me for their financial wellbeing gave me both a sense of pride and angst. I knew how much I missed out on as a child, emotionally and financially, and I was determined to make their lives better than mine had been. So, I did what I did best — I went to work.

I worked in every department at Menorah, including the morgue, where I assisted with autopsies and collected pathology specimens. I also stood at the operating table for hours and wrote daily reports each day for each department. My schedule was full, and I was lucky to get a few hours of sleep each night. But every path has its hardships, and when I felt like I had nothing left in the tank, it meant I had just enough to finish the job. Will power is a force to be reckoned with, and our minds and bodies are capable of more than we ever realize.

No Guts, No Glory

I made my way to Kansas and the Menorah Medical Center to train under Glen Reno. It was a risk to be sure, leaving Dixie and I both without a real job, but it paid off. Reno, as the administrator of the hospital, proved himself to be a powerful, dynamic man, and a great influence on me throughout my stay there. At age forty-five, he was a national leader in hospital administration. His way of solving seemingly insurmountable problems was to always look for that dynamic, outside-the-box solution. It became a strategy I used over and over again in my entrepreneurial ventures in the years to come.

Upon completing my residency at Menorah I obtained a staff position there. My career in hospital administration was moving ahead fast and furiously. Several years into my stay, however, Reno left the hospital to run his family's business. The man who succeeded him did not share the same principles and so I decided to leave shortly into his tenure. It was a difficult decision — weighing my values over my income — especially since Dixie and I had just recently become homeowners for the first time, but I knew I was doing the right thing.

Faced with a mortgage payment on an already overstretched, and now shrinking, budget, we were forced to find ways to make the most of every dollar. Dixie made the kids' clothing, canned and preserved fruits and vegetables, and refurbished old furniture — she was the consummate homemaker. She was a lifesaver, and a true life partner! I would need her support more than ever as I scrambled to find another job to support our family.

Closed Door, Open Window

I called one of my friends from the University of Minnesota,

Russ Miller, who was Executive Director at Kansas University Medical Center, and explained that I was looking for a new job. Russ was practically speechless at first. He told me that just the night before he'd been approached by Dr. Charles Gullett, Medical

 Director of TWA, regarding a new position they had just created.

TWA had just been awarded a contract from NASA and Gullett asked him if he knew anyone he could recommend for the job. Russ told him, "I only know one guy who could fill the position you are describing, and that's Jim Hindman." The timing couldn't have been better.

Russ gave me Dr. Gullett's phone number. I called him, set up at interview for later that day, met Dr. Gullett around one in the afternoon, and by five o'clock I had a new job — Director of Medical Administration of TWA/NASA.

Rocketing Ahead

By the late fifties, it was clear that the U.S. was losing the space exploration race to the Russians. After being elected in 1960, President Kennedy announced that the United States would send a man to the moon before the close of the sixties. Congress worked in concert with this announcement, passing legislation to fund space exploration, and national support for the

 program couldn't have been higher. The race was on! America wanted to win this one.

In the fall of 1963 I began work as director of the group that was assigned to open a medical center at

Cape Canaveral on Merritt Island, Florida. The task of developing the Occupational Health Program was huge, and I look back on it with pride. It was a great tribute to NASA's concern for the safety and care of all involved with the program. Their goal was to develop the best healthcare program possible, to deal with everything from the birth of the smallest baby to instant response to any accident or disaster.

In the summer of 1964 the medical team and the program were put to test. Unaware that the firing stage of a Delta rocket had just been joined to the Orbiting Solar Observatory satellite in a test building, someone accidentally pulled a shroud (a capsule cover) over the floor. This created a spark of static electricity within a chamber filled with pure oxygen, which started a fire that ignited the solid fuel in the third stage of the rocket. Three people died and eight others were severely burned in the resulting explosion. Our medical team was the first responder at this tragic scene, with the San Antonio Medical Burn Center team called in for assistance. It was a great and tragic loss, but also a testament to the work NASA had done to ensure the quick delivery of medical care to all its dedicated and distinguished employees.

The space program attracted people with great talent and capabilities. I was introduced to highly qualified professionals from all avenues of service and business. Because of the conglomeration of skills, knowledge, and abilities, the prevailing atmosphere at the Cape was electric! The sense of urgency resulting from our race with the Russians to The Moon created an attitude of "no excuses." Whatever the task, it was to be done, and done quickly. If a man could be sent into space and land on The Moon and return, surely the job, whatever it might be, could be done right, and right when it was needed.

Being part of a team to put a man on The Moon was a heady, whirlwind experience. It was "go, go, go," with all kinds of challenges and deadlines — the perfect environment for a Type A personality like me.

Nowhere to Go but Up?

University of Minnesota graduates were a tight-knit group who were always there to assist one another. Russ Miller had already helped me land the TWA/NASA gig, and now another alumnus, Walt Coburn, who was working as a hospital administration consultant in Kansas City, was looking to me for help. Walt called one day while I was still at the Space Center and asked if I would consider doing him a favor. There was a position available for a hospital administrator in Baltimore, Maryland, and he asked if I would interview for the job. He thought the hospital in question might be forced to close, and he didn't expect anyone to actually take the job, but he needed to interview candidates to fulfill his consultancy contract.

"Are you crazy?" I said. "I already have the best hospital administration job in the world. Why would I interview for a regular community hospital position? Thanks, but no thanks."

But, not long afterward, feeling guilty about refusing his request, I flew to Baltimore for the interview, and then promptly forgot about it.

A few days later, my secretary hurried into my office, interrupting a meeting, to announce that the vice president was on the phone. Thinking it was Dick Wilson of TWA, I said I'd call him back.

"No!" she said, "It's *the* Vice President!"

Confused, I picked up the phone. Thinking it was someone playing a joke, I asked rather gruffly, "Who is this?"

A laugh came from the other end, and I immediately recognized the distinctive voice of Hubert Humphrey.

Why would the Vice President of the United States be calling me? Humphrey continued, "I understand you visited Baltimore County General Hospital. I would really like to help these people out, and I have spoken with Dr. David Stoddard (TWA's boss on the Canaveral operation), and you will be hearing from him."

Whoa! By the time the conversation came to an end, Dick Wilson, TWA's VP, was at my door demanding to know what was going on. The whole Space Center was buzzing with the news. Soon I received a call from Dr. Stoddard, asking that I come to Washington to meet with him. Booked on the next flight to D.C., but still somewhat in the dark, I was on my way to NASA headquarters to meet with him.

Immediately, Dr. Stoddard reminded me that he reported to the Vice President, that he was the Director of NASA, that NASA was in charge of TWA's project, and that he was ultimately my boss. He went on, "So, young man, you've been elected to go to Baltimore County General Hospital and fill the Executive Director position."

I was in total shock, and even though I had a great job, how could I decline an offer from the Vice President of the United States? Besides, he practically made me a deal I couldn't refuse. Actually, it was a deal I would have been crazy to refuse. I would be a consultant to NASA, a consultant to TWA, *and* Executive Director of Baltimore County General Hospital. With a nod from the Vice President of the United States, it wasn't really a tough choice at all. And so, it was off to Baltimore.

CHAPTER 7
TAKING CARE OF OTHERS

Mission Accomplished

My charge at Baltimore County General was explicit. I was to run the hospital while accomplishing four primary objectives: improve the hospital's financial position; obtain a full-license (the hospital was operating on an appeal); receive Joint Commission accreditation; and get Blue Cross certification for the institution.

When I arrived, the hospital was on the brink of bankruptcy, so negotiations with the creditors were the first orders of business. I had to persuade them to accept fifty cents on the dollar for our outstanding debt — no simple challenge. The way I saw it, my only strategy was to be honest. I explained to our debtors that if the hospital was to survive, some significant financial restructuring was necessary. If they hoped to get something, they would have to be satisfied to take anything. Nearly every creditor agreed to my terms. Thus, my first objective was largely accomplished with little more than some friendly persuasion.

With the creditor problem successfully resolved, there was still the overdue second mortgage on the facility, and the holder was on the verge of pulling the plug. The hospital had no money to meet the obligation, and so the future of the hospital came down to an intense meeting between me and the bigwigs of the original mortgage holder, Loyola Savings and Loan. After I presented the hospital's case and answered all of the bank's questions, Sam Borden, the bank president, delighted with my presentation said, "See? I told you, all that place needed was the right management."

Looking down the long line of his troops at the big conference table, he went on, "Well, we've got this loan request for $75,000. What do you all think?"

One of his attorney advisors finally broke the silence, "Well, Mr. Borden, you know, it *is* illegal to grant a third party loan when there is an intervening second that we don't control."

Borden sharply retorted, "Have we ever done anything illegal before?" The room was completely silent, all eyes fixed squarely on the floor.

Borden slammed the table — BAM! "Give him the money!"

The paperwork was executed immediately, and not a minute too soon.

Check in hand, I met the second mortgage holder's representative on the courthouse steps on his way inside to get a judgment against us. And with that, the problem of the second mortgage was resolved.

Because of the faith Loyola Federal placed in me, it became a personal goal of mine to ensure the hospital repaid its debt. I was determined to demonstrate to Borden that when I said I was going to do something, I kept my word.

With the financial hurdles cleared, the other objectives were easily achieved. By November of 1968 I had accomplished all I was tasked to, and so I was free to leave.

Throughout my short time at Baltimore County General I expanded my consulting services, and by the time I left I had several government-related contracts with IBM, United Fruit, and other clients that would provide continuing consulting work in the management and healthcare fields. And, as always, I kept my eyes open for new opportunities.

Love Your Fellow Man

In graduate school, I wrote my thesis on elder care — current facilities and their environment, with a focus on improving care. My research for this project took me on visits to a number of nursing homes and state-operated facilities. On one such visit, the director of the facility was kind enough to take me on a full tour.

Making our way to the ward, at least a dozen patients in wheelchairs adorned the halls. The director expertly navigated the human maze, avoiding contact and interaction of every kind with these living monuments to the common human fate. I thought to myself, "These people are someone's parents, grandparents, wives, husbands…how did they get *here*?"

When we finally arrived in the main ward I simply couldn't believe what I saw. Seventy patients piled into what can only be described as a warehouse. It was heartbreaking.

The look on my face must have betrayed my feelings. The director turned to me and said, "Seven dollars a day. Seven bucks for each patient. We do what we can."

I faced my own mortality right then and there. Someday I would become just like these people — frail, dependent, pathetic. I knew that I never wanted to end up in a place like this. And I also knew that, if he were still alive, I would never have allowed Grandpa Wharton to live out his final days in such a miserable environment.

I thought to myself, "There has got to be a better way."

Doing It Better

It was about this time that the advent of Medicare and Medicaid was revolutionizing the nursing home industry. Because of new regulations, all nursing homes were required to have policy and procedure manuals as well as a licensed administrator. Up to this point, licensed nurses ran most nursing homes. It became apparent there was an unfilled need in this industry, and a wave of opportunity came with it. I began developing and writing policy and procedure manuals for small nursing homes as well as selling my administrative services. Based on my education, and professional and personal experiences, I was able to consult nursing homes on standards for delivering optimal care to their patients. All this was just the beginning of my vision for improving care for the elderly.

Expanding Horizons

One of my first clients when I began consulting with nursing homes was the Jewish Convalescent Home in Baltimore. There I met Jules Livingston, a board member who owned a pawnbroker business. Jules asked me if I could check out a facility located near Washington, D.C.

Evaluating facilities was part of my consulting business, and in the process of the inspection, I was introduced to Allen Berman. He was a self-made man. A bright, gutsy risk-taker, Berman got his start as a pawnbroker, but had successfully parlayed his way into the real estate investment business, leveraging and borrowing for expansion and growth.

The nursing home we toured was in Bethesda, Maryland. I knew a lot about the need for healthcare facilities in the area, and I confidently advised Berman to buy the business. A new wing had recently been added to the existing facility, and based on my recent demographic studies, I believed it could be filled quickly.

A few weeks later Berman called and asked, "If that nursing home in Bethesda is such a good deal, why don't you buy it?"

"Mr. Berman," I replied, "I couldn't write a check for $100, much less $100,000 for the down payment."

Berman knew that I knew what I was talking about when I recommended he buy the facility, but was also smart enough to know that he knew very little about nursing homes. With his money and my expertise, he was confident that this purchase would be a solid investment.

With some persuasion on his part, I agreed to join him the next day for a meeting at Providence Bank. He wanted to pursue the purchase of the nursing home in Bethesda and was offering me a chance to get in on the deal. He arranged a loan for me, which enabled me to put up $25,000 to buy into the home. Even though my part of the ownership was relatively small, due to my growing equity and the web of relationships I had developed and was developing, from that point on I had access to financial means that would allow me to pursue even more growth opportunities.

Doing It My Way

During my time at Baltimore County General Hospital, I met Dick Heacock, who served on the board of directors. He was a straightforward, somewhat abrupt, crusty guy with one blue eye and one brown, who loved to dance, play poker, and tip an occasional brew. Dick was a CPA and eventually served as my own personal accountant and advisor for many years. In the winter of 1969 he told me about an opportunity to purchase a nursing home. The owner was hoping to get out of the business in haste and I saw this as a great opportunity. So, with my mother-in-law Dorlean's assistance, we gave the owner a down payment on a contract to buy the land, the buildings, and the business. Within a few days of Dick first telling me about the opportunity, Dixie and

I became the owners of our very own nursing home — Chapel Hill Convalescent Home.

We lived right on the grounds of the small campus. The country setting provided a wonderful environment for our family, particularly during our children's pre-teen and teenage years. Dixie and I, our kids, the employees, the residents, we were like one big, extended family. And, most importantly, we were able to offer the type of compassionate and personal care that I felt was the responsibility of all caregivers to provide.

Risky Business

Not that my consulting work always provided a steady income, but owning and operating a nursing home, while emotionally satisfying, was particularly financially straining. Gone were the days of a regular paycheck. To me, this underscored the fact that it's difficult to have success and security in the same hand.

One morning very early into our venture, I awoke, worried sick. We had a two-week payroll to meet and absolutely no money to pay the employees. All our cash had been spent on the purchase of the home and the other typical expenses of operating a business.

As the day slogged on the problem was still unresolved, and I couldn't figure out how we could possibly obtain the money to fulfill our payroll obligations. But, if we didn't, our exit from the nursing home industry would be quicker than our entry. Beaten down, I sat slumped behind the desk in my office, when out of the blue a lawyer walked in. He asked me if we would consider $25,000 for a life-care contract for one of his clients — to take care of her for the rest of her life. Can do! Problem solved. We were saved. Not a day went by that I didn't say hello to that little lady and give her a giant hug from my heart of hearts.

Up and Out

In time, Dixie began singlehandedly running Chapel Hill while also raising our children, which allowed me to continue expanding our nursing home portfolio with Allen Berman. From our first home in Bethesda, we continued to increase our ownership stakes throughout Maryland, and into Nebraska, Iowa, and Illinois. A healthcare operation that was looking to improve its asset position before going public took note of our flourishing empire and made us a substantial offer to buy us out. Thus, after a little less than a decade in the nursing home business, I had accomplished all and more than I had set out to. Dixie and I had purchased a facility together and were able to give great care to deserving patients. And, through some timely associations, I was able to grow a business and walk away with a sizeable profit. In fact, Berman and I made so much money on the buy-out that I officially retired at just 35! From an orphan to a millionaire — ain't it great!

CHAPTER 8
NOW WHAT?

Everyone Needs a Cause and a Purpose

"Do you realize how lucky you are?" Berman asked, "Thirty-five years old and already a millionaire."

Up to this point in my life the thought that I was, would be, could be, a millionaire had never crossed my mind. I always enjoyed a challenge, and I performed at my best when I had a purpose. Reflecting on my life, I realized that all along I was always aiming for something.

From my earliest days I was focused on survival, and trying to make life better for my little brothers. At the Boys and Girls Home I was looking to uncover who I was and all my potential. Throughout high school and college I set out to be the best football player I could be, and eventually the best student I could be, all with the hope of making something of myself. When I met Dixie I knew I had met the person whom I wanted to start a family with and to share my life with. I strived to do my best in the business world, accomplishing all that was expected of me at TWA/NASA, at Baltimore County General, and in my consulting work. I saw a need in the healthcare field, and helped to deliver quality care to patients in nursing homes. And, in the end, all these pursuits culminated in me gaining financial independence with the accompanying luxury of no longer having to work. I didn't mean to become a millionaire, it just kind of happened as I set out to accomplish what I felt I needed to do.

As I considered Berman's comments more deeply, and all that I had achieved, I thought to myself, "Is this really all there is?"

Money really hadn't changed anything in my life. Sure, I felt a little better about myself — that I had accomplished so much. And, of course, I was glad to know that my wife and children would be well provided for. But somehow life just didn't seem any different, especially since the only thing that was different was a few more zeroes on my bank statement each month.

"A millionaire," I thought to myself, "So what?!"

I was unsettled. My whole life to that point had been spent on a mission. Now I had none. I knew I had to do something; I couldn't just rest in my past accomplishments. I needed to be involved. I needed a challenge.

It was time for a change.

One of Those Moments

The first step in finding my new purpose was to get away. I decided to take a family vacation, and in the process, find some time to seclude myself and think about what my new mission might be.

We went to the deserts of Arizona, an ideal place to withdraw, take in the world, and to just think. High up on a dune, marveling at the never-ending expanse of the rolling sands, BAM! The answer hit me like a ton of bricks.

My life was the product of the influences of a large web of great teachers and coaches. On my own I couldn't have made it. But because of the time, patience, encouragement, and investment of so many, I achieved more than anyone would have ever imagined. And now it was my turn to contribute to others, to give back. I decided to turn back to my first love. I decided to coach football, to teach a group of young men the lessons I was so fortunate to receive years before.

I reflected on my earliest coaching experiences. When our kids were old enough to start getting involved in sports, our son Tim joined a Little League football team, and I was the assistant coach. I am sure I enjoyed it more than he did. On top of some father and son bonding, I simply thrived on teaching those little guys the fundamentals — offensive and defensive plays, the rules of the game, discipline, sportsmanship, and the importance of teamwork. I felt revitalized while sharing with them the principles that could ultimately become their playbooks for life, both on and off the field. I subsequently parlayed that coaching experience into a job as a volunteer football coach at the Community College of Baltimore County. So, this new coaching job, wherever it would be, would not be my first.

A few days after returning home from our trip to Arizona, Dixie and I were invited to a friend's house for dinner. I was recounting my epiphany to one of the other guests, a graduate of Western Maryland College, telling him that I was thinking of joining the coaching staff at Johns Hopkins University. He didn't let me finish. "No, no...a thousand times no!" he responded. "You've got to come to Western Maryland College!"

"The Millionaire Coach"

When he told me about the possibility of coaching at Western Maryland — or rather insisted I take my knowledge and passions there — I knew very little about the college. I decided to investigate

and made an appointment to visit the campus. While waiting to be shown into the head coach's office, I noticed the memorabilia displayed in a cabinet nearby — it was all football. This was my kind of place! By the end of the day, I was hired as the assistant football coach at the college. One year later, I was appointed head football coach, and they certainly couldn't beat the price...one dollar a year!

In my first season, when I was the assistant coach, the team won 2 and lost 7. By the third year we reversed that, finishing with an 8-2 record. I never set out to win games, I simply presented the players with a strategy to help them become winners. Plan, organize, and control was our motto. With that I was able to help the players grow mentally, physically, and spiritually, and because of this growth and our commitment to planning and executing we became winners naturally.

My appointment opened avenues for me to participate in seminars and coaching clinics, including a stroke of good fortune, an opportunity to learn from one of the masters, the great Coach Bear Bryant. Without a doubt, coaching provided more fun and satisfaction for me than any of my previous life ventures.

I will always be grateful to Dr. Ralph John, president of Western Maryland College, for giving me the opportunity to coach there for five years. I was honored with two coaching awards in 1978, Middle Atlantic Conference Coach of the Year and the Board of Governors Award of the Touchdown Club of Washington, D.C. Even though I was thrilled to receive this recognition, it was an even greater thrill to have five WMC players awarded Division III All-American status during my coaching years. For me, coaching was always about giving the players my best in order to help bring out the best in them.

CHAPTER 9
SOMETHING OUT OF NOTHING

The Challenge

I showed my players at Western Maryland College that with hard work and dedication they could achieve anything. To me, coaching isn't about making people into something they aren't. It's about making them into everything they already are, even though they might not know it yet. It's about showing people their potential, pushing them to reach it, and then getting out of the way so they will know that it was their effort, and not mine, that got them there.

Our success on the football field lent a sense of pride to the entire student body at WMC. It also built for me a reputation as someone who demanded a lot from his players, but who was also able to get the most out of them. In short, people respected me for my successes, both on and off the field, and understood that my guidance and advice would always be honest, firm, and usually (hopefully) helpful. So, players and students would often come to my office for counsel on any number of problems or concerns. I wasn't surprised, then, when a student came into the office one April day in 1978.

That fateful visit, a graduating senior slumped down in one of the hard, high-backed wooden chairs in front of my desk.

"What can I do for you?" I asked.

He got right to the point, "I guess I'm just gonna have to apply for a job at Social Security; there's nothing out there. It's not like it was for you...things've changed."

Totally amazed and somewhat amused, I immediately shot back, "What are you talking about? What are those pinko bastards teaching you over there anyway? That's ridiculous! I grew up during the Depression — you bet things have changed! When I was your age, I saw opportunities everywhere and it's no different today. America is still America and there are plenty of opportunities for those who want them, and that means you, too, Jack!"

Totally unmoved, he replied, "I bet you couldn't do it again."

He meant, of course, I bet you couldn't make a million dollars again. With that, the challenge was on, and I let him know that I had accepted it right then and there.

"Let me tell you something, not only can I do it again, but I'm going to take a whole bunch of your classmates with me!"

Gauntlet thrown. Game on.

This exchange hit me hard, and it lit a fire within me. I was about to embark on a yearlong mission in order to prove that the free enterprise system was alive and well.

Filling a Need

I began to search for opportunities. No matter which market niche I examined, I always seemed to return to the idea of franchising. It was a way for people to be in business for themselves, yet at the same time, receive assistance from teammates — the corporate franchisor, fellow franchisees, and the International Franchise Association. But what should the franchise be? I found the answer through a stroke of luck, both bad and good.

I had one of my football players take my car for an oil change. Unable to get it serviced at a gas station, he took it to a local car dealership. When he returned to pick it up, he found the dashboard removed, broken, and lying on the front seat. Apparently, work orders had gotten mixed up, and in turn, I got a broken dash and someone else got my oil change! The dealership service station said it would be at least three more days before the car would be repaired.

I thought to myself, "There's got to be a better way!"

Months later, I came across a magazine with the headline, "Best and Hottest Business Prospects for the 80's." Perhaps because of my recent oil change mishap, one of the ideas hooked my attention: "Make $100,000 a year in quick oil changes." The article featured an entrepreneur in Utah who had started a business of doing oil changes and a few maintenance checks without an appointment. The concept of a business specializing in convenient oil changes made great sense to me, and my intuition told me to look deeper into it.

I began to study the oil change market. Clearly a window of opportunity was opening fast. More than a hundred thousand corner gas stations were closing. The big oil companies' need to create greater cash flow was prompting them to convert the corner gas stations into pumping stations with self-service only. But regular oil changes were still vital to maintaining the life of cars and trucks. The ever-smaller car engines needed more frequent changes, people were keeping their cars longer, and both spouses working usually meant multiple vehicles in a household. All of this only upped the importance of and need for oil changes.

An oil change that was fast, convenient, and reasonably priced could possibly be the business I was looking for. I began discussing the idea with Ed Kelley, one of my assistant coaches at Western Maryland, as well as some other friends and mentors. My enthusiasm increased during a conversation with my brother-in-law, Chuck Hobbs, who had recently learned of another quick-lube business in Colorado, operating under the name of "Jiffy Lube." Chuck paid it a visit, and after hearing about his tour of a clean, efficient operation that provided a quick oil change, with no appointment necessary, I got even more excited. Apparently, the owner of the Colorado station had gone into business after purchasing a Jiffy Lube franchise from a man named Edward Washburn.

Washburn lived in Utah where he developed the idea of Jiffy Lube in 1970. So, Ed Kelley and I flew out there to tour other Jiffy Lube units in Salt Lake and Ogden. We reviewed the Jiffy Lube business model — the start-up costs, financing plan, suppliers, everything. What was perhaps most innovative about his operation was that his stores had full basements, which enabled employees to quickly serve regular vehicles and also oversized vehicles like RVs. He had also developed procedures to service vehicles within ten minutes, including topping off fluids, vacuuming the interior, and washing the exterior windows — and all that for just $12.95, with no appointment necessary.

As our departure time drew near, I decided to shift my plan of only buying the rights to own and operate Jiffy Lube franchises in the State of Maryland to buying the entire company! I wanted everything — the concept, trademarks, trade names, the operational secrets and systems, the national contracts, and, of course, the agreements Washburn had with his small family of franchisees. After a restless night considering our best approach, I asked Washburn point blank if he'd sell me the whole company.

He definitely wasn't ready for that! After composing himself, discussions began and a deal was made. On May 24, 1979, Jiffy Lube International, Inc. was formed and on June 2, 1979, at our first Board of Directors meeting, Jiffy Lube International, Inc. acquired the Jiffy Lube assets from me.

It Takes a Team

From the beginning, we laid the foundation for the Jiffy Lube culture and philosophy, for our way of doing business. Our first team meeting became our first annual convention for all the franchisees, including all the Jiffy Lube stakeholders — product suppliers, equipment vendors, investors, and anyone interested in joining us on our journey. There I laid out a basic philosophy for our operation: the three "I's," *Intensity, Integrity,* and *Intimacy.* We would become known as a hard-working, trustworthy, passionate team.

Our commitment to excellence later became a part of our annual conventions in what we called the "Best There Is" contest. Delivering outstanding service to each and every customer was our goal. In our way of doing things, the training and commitment of our lube technicians and unit managers contributed the most to the growth and acceptance of the Jiffy Lube concept within each market we entered.

After regular shop hours, Jiffy Lube teams would practice, honing their skills to deliver top-notch oil changes in ten minutes or less. The teams within the four regions of the country competed and the final four winners would then compete at our annual convention for the coveted title. It was a thrill to watch these folks deliver a "jiffy lube" with such efficiency, skill, and professionalism. A Super Bowl team wins a trophy and all team members proudly sport a ring. Well, our Super Jiffy

Lubers were no exception, they were, after all, "The Best There Is"!

Growing Pains

It was the 1980s and the prime interest rate was on its way to 21.5%. Long-term real estate financing rates were a whopping 18.5%! We were heading into the jaws of the recession of 1980 – 1982, considered at the time to be the most severe of the post-WWII recessions. We were not only faced with economic challenges, but the Jiffy Lube concept was still relatively unknown. Regardless of the economic foreboding, the more we studied the quick-lube industry, the more convinced we were that the market potential was far bigger than we first believed.

Seeing this potential, we were sure others would soon follow. So, we created a plan for expansion — to be the first and to be the biggest. But, with the company in its infancy and the country in recession, getting access to capital to build new stores was out of the question. Our only alternative, then, was growth through acquisitions. We leveraged ourselves considerably and quickly grew to twenty-nine centers, with system-wide sales by the year's end of $2.5 million. Not bad for our second year in operation.

As extended as we were after our initial acquisitions we knew if we were to become a viable franchise we would need to continue to grow. And we knew if we were to continue to grow we would need capital. Enter Pennzoil.

The Proposal

Before seriously considering getting into the quick-lube business I diligently studied all I could about it. My studies only increased as we continued to grow the Jiffy Lube brand. Through my research I learned that, on the east coast, from Rhode Island

68

to Maryland, Quaker State dominated the market, having nearly 30% market share. Far below them was Pennzoil, at just 2%. Inspiration struck.

If I could convince Pennzoil that Jiffy Lube was the vehicle for increasing their market share they might be willing to help finance our, and so their, growth. It was worth a shot.

We discussed the plan with Pennzoil's vice president of national sales, and the possibility of presenting a financing proposal to the president of Pennzoil. Ultimately, a meeting was arranged. Arriving in Houston, we were ushered into Pennzoil's oversized executive area and I gave my pitch.

"Quaker State owns 27% of the market. You guys own 2%. How'd you like to reverse that?"

I had their attention.

I unfolded my plan, how securing $1,000,000 in equity investment and millions more in real estate financing from them would allow Jiffy Lube to open new stores and expand into new territories, and how the more stores there were using Pennzoil for the oil changes the more oil Pennzoil would obviously sell, and so the greater their market share would be. It was a picture-perfect presentation, but the honchos weren't sold.

Seeing that my vision for Pennzoil's future had not completely captivated the audience, I gathered my thoughts and walked confidently to the head of the table where Wayne Warren, Pennzoil's president, was seated. His oversized leather executive chair swung to meet me.

"Mr. Warren," I said deferentially, as I fell to one knee as if to propose, my hands cupped in front of me, ready to receive whatever pity he might spare, "Will you *please* give us a million dollars?"

Silence.

Warren eased back in his chair, looked towards the far corner of the room, sighed, and finally looked back at me.

"Ok, Jim, we'll give you the money."

Sold! And what a sale it was. Deal made, $1,000,000 check in hand! Jiffy Lube International was now officially off and running with future stores slated to display the Pennzoil name, use the Pennzoil brand, all the while relying on Pennzoil capital!

In the months that followed, with a cooperative effort between the two companies, more independent quick-lube chains were acquired and brought into the Jiffy Lube family.

All in the Family

To my promise, I recruited former Western Maryland players to be part of Jiffy Lube's management team and to become independent franchisees. Many of our franchise sales were the result of long-established business relationships, as well as members of our own management and staff who left the comforts of salaried jobs to become entrepreneurs — Jiffy Lube franchisees. Seeing the courage of these young men and women as they ventured forth was not only exciting and satisfying for me, but their efforts spread the Jiffy Lube culture and philosophy throughout the franchise network, and also to our stakeholders, investors, and board members.

All those who believed in us and joined us early on were vital to our success. Together we shaped the Jiffy Lube culture that became our differentiator as we faced competitors with far greater financial resources.

With things moving very quickly within the company, regrettably, I was now forced to say goodbye to my football coaching. My commitment to the franchise owners could not be compromised.

It would take all of my mind, heart, and resources, if we were to compete with the major oil companies and catapult Jiffy Lube to a national brand.

Sign of the Times

Jiffy Lube was now into its fourth year, and with one hundred units open, we certainly had proved the legitimacy of our franchise. Our goal would turn now toward building a national brand, and eventually becoming a publicly held company.

With this grandiose goal in mind, we took a giant leap forward in our branding strategy and hired Lois Pitts Gershon, a New York advertising firm, whose contribution to the creation of the Jiffy Lube brand was immeasurable. LPG was headed by the creative genius George Lois who created the "J arrow" logo that today, more than thirty years later, still identifies Jiffy Lube and its brand of excellence.

Bad Debt

To grow into a national company Jiffy Lube needed to expand rapidly. The problem was, expansion devours capital, and so we needed money. To meet our financial needs we entered into a multi-million dollar loan agreement with Old Court Savings & Loan of Baltimore.

Continuing to pursue our acquisition strategy, in January 1985 we were presented with an opportunity to acquire a quick-lube chain of some fifty units in the Chicago area with additional units in St. Louis, Missouri, and Houston, Texas. Despite Jiffy Lube's expansion into the Chicago market, our celebration was brief. Our lives were about to be turned upside down.

On May 6, 1985, *Baltimore Sun* headlines announced: "OLD

COURT SEIZED." The timing couldn't have been worse. Our loan agreement with Old Court was providing millions for construction of multiple Jiffy Lube units as well as monies for the purchase of new sites. Within one week of the announcement, we were informed that all of our funding had been cut off. Within four months of placing Old Court in receivership, we received a notice from the State of Maryland, demanding the payback of two and one-half million dollars that had been funded by Old Court prior to the State's takeover of it.

From day one we had made it clear to all the Jiffy Lube team players that we were in this adventure together. All of the members were aware of the national crisis in the Savings and Loan industry that had forced the seizure of Old Court, and the president of the Jiffy Lube Association of Franchisees suggested that we seek some funding from the franchisees. Within weeks, they had loaned us several million dollars. With team players like this, I was more determined than ever to lead the company through this crisis.

Promise Kept

Even before I met Ed Washburn for the first time in 1979, I felt that Jiffy Lube, with its ten-minute oil change concept, could become the McDonald's of the quick-lube industry. To that vision, on July 22, 1986, Jiffy Lube became a publicly held company with a 2,033,000 share offering at $15.00 per share. The stock closed at $21.25. What a day we had! Nearly twenty members of the Jiffy Lube team became overnight millionaires. And Jiffy Lube would soon become the household word for an oil change.

Within a year of becoming a public company, with stock prices rising, the company entered into a $100 million real estate deal with Pennzoil. It seemed like nothing could stop us. Of course, it only seemed that way.

Write-Offs

In late summer of 1987, we were hit with bad news from our audit firm. Because of a change in FASB (Financial Accounting Standards Board) regulations, we had to reduce a portion of our reported earnings from over $5 million to a little more than $100,000. For a public company — for any company — that's huge! As a result, the stock price plummeted, but we survived.

We continued to expand with the help of Pennzoil and in March of 1988 Jiffy Lube and Pennzoil signed a "strategic alliance." This quasi-partnership made sense for both companies. After all, Jiffy Lube and Pennzoil shared a common goal. The Jiffy Lube system, through acquisitions and continued growth, had increased Pennzoil's oil distribution market. The success of one meant success for the other.

In August of 1988 we opened our one-thousandth unit in Raleigh, North Carolina. Growing to that many centers in a few short years had taken its toll and stretched our resources to their limits. Jiffy Lube's leadership position in the quick-lube industry had come at a big financial price, given the many millions needed for real estate financing coupled with the reality that many of our franchisees were in their infancy operationally. In short, Jiffy Lube was leveraged in a major way. Any surprises and the entire company would be in danger.

The nearly five million dollar write-down was still looming at year's end, and as the accounting review progressed, the proverbial "other shoe" dropped. Additional accounting rules, the result of the Savings and Loan crisis, were creating an even larger write-off, and I was advised the loss would be much greater than originally anticipated. When the smoke cleared, there was an estimated write-off of 35 – 38 million dollars in earnings. Now, the proverbial "camel's back" was about to break.

By early 1989, the review was complete and the strict Security Exchange Commission rules stipulated that in any publicly held company, information, either good or bad, must be reported to everyone simultaneously. There were lenders – hundreds of millions of dollars had been provided to us over the past years, including franchisees who had invested their entire life savings in their Jiffy Lube centers – Jiffy Lube employees numbering in the thousands, landlords, supplies, and then there was Pennzoil. We had obligations to many...I had obligations to many.

Therefore, on Valentine's Day 1989 we released a nationally distributed announcement regarding our write-offs. Our board of directors and key advisors had already met, and the decision was made to include in the press release that Jiffy Lube was exploring strategic alternatives —street talk for an acquisition.

It was an emotional roller coaster as we tried to figure out the right strategy for the Jiffy Lube family's future. Of all the options discussed, failure wasn't one of them. Still, as our stock continued to plummet and as leveraged as we were, we had to do something.

The Final Step

Financial turmoil forced us to make some difficult decisions. But the solution to our problems was closer than we first realized. Pennzoil! We had counted on them since the very beginning and their investment in us had benefited both our companies. It only made sense, then, to take the final step in what seemed inevitable from the beginning anyway.

On January 3rd, 1990, the *Baltimore Sun* business headline

read, "Jim Hindman, ex-football coach and entrepreneur who helped father the $10 billion quick-lube industry, is passing the baton to Pennzoil Company."

A Legacy

Today, Jiffy Lube is one of the most recognized brands in America. (*Entrepreneur* magazine ranked Jiffy Lube among the top three franchises in its Franchise 500 listing for 2013.) With over 2,400 centers, it is one of the largest automotive service companies in the world. It has been part of many business school case studies in this country. Over 40,000 people are employed in the Jiffy Lube system today; over one billion dollars is generated in revenues; and nearly thirty million vehicles serviced every year.

During the ten years of growing Jiffy Lube, we survived four recessions, interest rates of over twenty percent, record-high unemployment, three stock market collapses, and every form of competition possible. And all this because of a dare and a dream.

In the end, I had fulfilled another mission — proving that America's free enterprise system was alive and well, and that possibility still existed if a person was willing to look for it and work at it. Still, I wasn't ready to rest. I needed a new challenge.

CHAPTER 10
SOMETHINGS OUT OF NOTHINGS

Why Don't You Do Something about It

After Jiffy Lube, I was fifty-five years old and looking for my next challenge. Retirement, again, was obviously not an option. In 1991, as I was considering my next mission, I received a call from the governor of Maryland, my good friend Donald Schaefer. Aware of my business successes and my fondness for coaching and inspiring youth, Schaefer persuaded me to attend a conference in D.C. on a crisis that the country was facing — the rise of school dropouts, alcohol and drug abuse, and other similar trends of delinquency. The morning agenda moved along painfully slow with few, if any, practical or even thoughtful solutions being offered. Obviously, this enclave of Washington elite stood miles, universes, apart from the problems and realities these young people faced. But, I knew firsthand the troubles of these youth — I had lived them.

If this was to be a conference about kids, under the auspices that it was about the wellbeing of kids, then someone actually had to speak up on their behalf. During the lunch break, I tracked down the leader of the conference, introduced myself, and asked him why the agenda had failed to include discussion on the needs of and plans for adjudicated youth — those kids who had committed delinquent offenses, but whose sentences called for something other than, usually less than, direct and collateral consequences (i.e. prison sentences). The man, clearly bothered by my reproach, bluntly responded,

"Frankly, we've written them off, and I think it would be best if you didn't bring this up again, okay?"

With that, he made leave of my unwelcome company.

I was flabbergasted and furious. How could a group of kids in this great nation just be "written off"?

I took my report back to the governor, spending most of the time animatedly recounting my exchange with the icy conference leader. He politely nodded, but said little. After about ten minutes of me ranting and the governor giving little more than the occasional token "uh-huh," I stepped down from my soapbox, unsure how my message was received.

"Well Jim..." he began, quite impatiently, "Why don't you do something about it?"

It was much more of a challenge than a question made in passing. And it was all I needed to be propelled into yet another entrepreneurial venture. Youth Services International, Inc. became my new mission, my new commitment. If no one wanted these kids, I would take them!

Another Chance

Not long after our meeting, the governor arranged for my daughter Cindi (a pediatrician with a doctorate in Child Development and Behavioral Science) and me to visit The Charles H. Hickey School, a state-operated facility for Maryland's adjudicated youth located northwest of Baltimore known for its long history of treatment and management problems.

What we witnessed there was disturbing, to say the least. There was no attempt being made to rehabilitate the kids. No programs existed to change their thinking or attitudes. The educational and vocational training curricula were substandard at best, and it was apparent that many of the kids were being unnecessarily medicated. In other words, the whole population was basically being swept under the rug. They were just serving their time.

I gave a detailed and honest report to Schaefer. He continued to stay in touch and a few months later told me that he was putting together a bus tour for a group of politicians and businessmen to visit a reportedly well-run facility in Concordville, Pennsylvania, called Glen Mills School. I readily agreed to join them. The governor wanted to see if we could create a similar program at Hickey School, and I was eager to see for myself how a quality facility operated.

Glen Mills was a non-profit organization that provided rehabilitation programs for both in-state and out-of-state adjudicated youth. As we drove onto their nicely manicured campus, we saw no bars on the windows or high barbed wire fences surrounding the perimeters, as was customary in Maryland's institutions. The buildings and facilities were neat, clean, and well maintained. The facility's behavioral change and educational programs created a positive peer culture that held each young man accountable for his actions, as well as for confronting fellow students who violated the rules or demonstrated unacceptable behavior.

Their holistic rehabilitative approach, based on trust, accountability, and personal growth, was improving behaviors and attitudes and treating addiction problems, as well as providing a top-notch educational and training program for all the students. Observing the students and staff busy in classrooms, workshops, libraries, and sports activities, showed us that this program was providing a healthy avenue for kids to turn their lives around, regardless of their background or history. The young people were treated as adults with the potential for achieving successful futures.

I realized then that I had been called to the perfect challenge. I had firsthand experience that I could use to give back to society in the same way that so many had given to me. I had a vision, a plan, and the knowledge and motivation to capitalize on them.

Plan, Organize, Control

As always, my approach was to put together a talented team with expertise in all the areas required. We needed to consider every facet of caring for and rehabilitating these kids — twenty-four hour staffing, meals and menus that met nutritional guidelines, a state-certified educational curriculum, medical care, athletic programs, weekend activity schedules, security procedures, cost projections, state and health department inspections, progress reports on students, and more. In short, our plan would have to cover everything, especially the 24/7/365 care of the youth.

The plan for what we called Youth Services International was developed and a proposal written in a small storefront location in Glyndon, Maryland, by a team that had experience and expertise in youth counseling, psychology, government laws and regulations, nutrition, building and architectural engineering requirements, finance, and security. The team included retired military leadership, successful businessmen, bank executives, CPAs, and attorneys working tirelessly for six months.

Our mission was to help some good kids who had done bad things rebuild their lives. There was a need to provide educational "catch-up," as most of the students lagged behind their grade level, and we also wanted to expose the students to, and train them for, what we called the world of work. We needed to teach them many things that might seem pretty mundane as well, such as manners and proper social conduct. Youth Services International was all about helping these kids reach their potential and providing them with the tools they needed to succeed. Now, all we needed was a facility where we could implement our vision.

Back Home

When our proposal was rejected and we lost our first bid to enact our plan at The Hickey School, we decided to take what we considered an excellent program elsewhere.

Early in the start-up of Youth Services International, I had an interview with the *Des Moines Register* regarding YSI and its mission. It caught the eye of Cindy Cox, the Executive Director of Economic Development in Clarinda, Iowa.

Clarinda is a small, idyllic town in southwestern Iowa with a large state-owned mental health facility built in 1885. At one point this facility had served as many as 1,500 patients, but as patient occupancy declined, the facility was slated for closure. If it were closed, there would be a loss of employment and negative economic repercussions through the community.

Multiple meetings with state legislators, judges, juvenile justice officers and administrators, and other interested parties followed in an effort to explain our program and answer questions. We made it clear that we weren't interested in just warehousing kids for a period of time. Our goal was to help change and redirect the lives of young people who had made some poor choices. We won the bid and YSI was officially in business. And what irony. I was back in Iowa, but this time I was the one offering kids a way out.

Time to Execute

The plans and programs we so carefully outlined and wrote for our Hickey School bid were no longer just blueprints. They were marching orders for YSI. Could we make money on our philosophy? I knew we could, while saving the taxpayers money, helping a whole bunch of kids, and reforming the system in the process.

The program was fortunate to attract a highly skilled staff. Many of them had military backgrounds and years of experience that not only contributed to the program, but provided great role models for the students. With something of a boot camp approach, the students were up at the crack of dawn. With a rigorous exercise schedule and an equally rigorous academic schedule and activities, they were propelled from one activity to another. There was little time or energy left over at the end of the day to brood over past injustices or to plot escapes. The Marine Corps was not the only one operating on the premise that less free time meant less time for trouble. The exclusive and expensive New England prep schools also used tightly controlled schedules. Our program was no different than that of the "privileged" whose parents were paying many thousands of dollars a year for this type of structured care.

Expanding Our Impact

Finding existing facilities with surrounding acreage or privately owned facilities that were looking to merge with a larger company was YSI's philosophy and business plan for expansion and growth. And that is exactly what we did. Over a six year period, YSI grew to include other programs in Iowa, Maryland, Michigan, Virginia, Florida, Arizona, Tennessee, Missouri, and South Dakota.

Personal Influence

Every company or organization has successes, but I believe YSI's successes are perhaps best measured by the letters and notes received from students, parents, and others who experienced or witnessed transformational change thanks to the school. What a tribute to the entire YSI team!

A student wrote:

"Entering the academy 7½ months ago, I went from an attitude of…'I need to know whatever it takes to get out of here' to…'I need to be here as long as it takes me to get my life back on track.' Sacrificing a few months of my young adult life is well worth the benefits I reaped. Today, I see myself as a responsible, motivated, ambitious person, but best of all…I see a person who takes responsibility for his actions and owns the consequences, something that person never used to do."

A parent:

"Before entering your facility, my daughter was involved in gangs, very cold, manipulative, lied, and even stole from her own family, feeling no guilt for the things she was doing. In your program, she learned very quickly to take responsibility, including responsibility for her behavior and accepting the fact there were consequences. Upon completion of your program, she attended a private school that was strict and required her to study and concentrate. She completed high school and is now in college, making a 4.0 average in Civil Engineering."

Another parent:

"Our son returned from your academy as a young man

*who is intelligent and interesting…one we are enjoying
getting to know all over again. He is also very considerate
and respectful toward his family. I want to thank you
for all the help you have given our son and most recently
his achievement with the ACT exam."*

A juvenile court officer:

*"I am writing to express my reaction to your program and
facility. The young man I placed in your academy six weeks
ago and met on my recent visit were two completely
different individuals. Upon entering the academy he had
very low self-esteem, was totally unmotivated, and did
not present or express himself well. Today, I saw a young
man who was well groomed, confident, expressive,
and motivated. It is refreshing to witness a program that
takes a young man with delinquent behaviors and
turns him into a trusting and trustable individual.
I congratulate and thank you."*

For me, the YSI venture was about much more than business.
It was personal. In those kids, I saw a fate I might have shared
had it not been for the positive impact of several caring people in
my own life. So, I was invested in the youth and I joined them in
their activities. We went camping, whitewater rafting, and fishing.
I relished the chance to give them things they didn't have, to do
things with them they had never done, and might never do again.
I think the difference between YSI and my other careers was that
level of personal identity with the kids at the academies. It was
easy for me to see what should be done to redirect them and
place them on the road to success. I had a model to follow, and

that model was me!

As the years rolled by, the company continued to grow and it brought us all great satisfaction to know that we were making a real difference in the lives of many troubled kids. Little did I know that I was about to face troubles of my own.

---

*"**D**eep in the Catoctin Mountains, just over the hill from central Maryland's Camp David Presidential retreat, 58-year-old W. James Hindman strides purposefully along the tree-lined paths of what could easily be mistaken for a summer camp. It's not. Surrounding much of the compound is an imposing 18-foot fence. And the teenagers who sidle up to Hindman as he makes his way to the main administration building are here because they have been convicted of burglary, assault, and drug trafficking. This is a reform school called the Victor Cullen Academy. Jim Hindman is the boss. 'They respect me because I'm strong,' Hindman says. 'I get things done.'*

"Cullen Academy is but 1 of 13 facilities nationwide that Hindman has bundled into a company called Youth Services International Inc. (YSI). In February, he took it public, and now holds 31% of the stock."

Bloomberg Business Week

CHAPTER 11
THE CALM BEFORE THE STORM

Surprise!

I discovered what macular degeneration was completely by accident. It was 1992. I was fifty-seven, and deeply engrossed in YSI. It was during this time my wife Dixie learned that her mother in Whiting, Iowa was experiencing trouble with her vision. Dorlean was satisfied with the treatment she was receiving, but I wanted to make sure she was getting the best care possible. So, I flew her into Maryland to get examined by the world-renowned doctors at the Wilmer Eye Institute at Johns Hopkins.

The Wilmer Eye Institute at Johns Hopkins, founded in 1925 and located in Baltimore, Maryland, is an internationally recognized eye institution that specializes in the diagnosis and management of eye diseases involving complex medical and surgical treatment. The largest department of ophthalmology in the United States, Wilmer is also regarded as a national leader in research and in the training of medical students, residents, fellows, and ophthalmic technicians.

A Date with Destiny

Despite my encouragement, Dorlean was reluctant to go. In addition to the fear we all have at times of a doctor looking into something that's been bothering us, Hopkins was a huge institution which, for someone who came from a small rural town that didn't have a hospital, only added to her hesitation. So I volunteered to go with her. Not just go the hospital with her, which I was obviously going to do anyway, but to have my eyes examined as well. I wanted her to feel secure, to know that she wasn't alone.

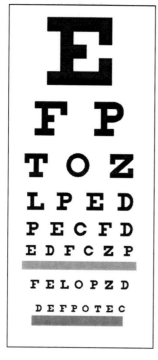

So we had our exams. The doctors at Wilmer were completely happy with the treatment Dorlean was receiving, and told us there was nothing they would do differently to treat her macular degeneration. "So, *that's* what she has," I thought to myself, still unsure what that meant. That was not the end of their prognosis however.

As I waited for my dilated pupils to return to normal, Dr. Morton Goldberg, head of Wilmer, delivered the shocking news — *I* was showing signs of macular degeneration, too! Well, I didn't expect that!

I knew something about my mother-in-law's symptoms, but to this point I didn't really know anything about the disease. After Goldberg explained it to me, I just couldn't believe I had a disease that could make me go blind. After all, I didn't have any symptoms I was aware of — my vision was near perfect. So, even though he said it was so, to me, that didn't make it so.

Despite Goldberg's explanations and my familiarity with Dorlean's worsening vision, I didn't really understand or accept the implications of my diagnosis or the disease in general. Somewhere along the line in my rough-and-tumble childhood I got the idea that nobody could hurt me. Naturally, I figured this couldn't either.

Ignorance is Bliss

Through the many trials and errors of my educational and professional careers I discovered the power of knowledge. The more I knew, the more I could do. When I encountered something unfamiliar or interesting in the business world, I launched right into educating myself about it. I tracked down and read anything about it I could get my hands on, I went to conferences and events, I completely immersed myself in learning all I could.

With macular degeneration, for some reason, I didn't do any of that. In fact, I didn't even mention the diagnosis to anyone outside my immediate family. I was involved in securing a major contract for Youth Services International, and, I suppose, that was my main and only focus. Regardless of my business priorities, however, I felt that whatever macular degeneration did to other people, it wasn't going to do to me. I had overcome every hurdle and obstacle that ever stood in my way. Macular degeneration would be no different.

Little did I know, however, that macular degeneration is a formidable opponent, and, as it would turn out, one I greatly underestimated. Over the course of the next twenty years, this disease would not only rob me of my sight, but impact my life in many unimagined and unexpected ways.

CHAPTER 12
A DREAM COME TRUE

Farming Life for Me

My diagnosis of macular degeneration passed quickly out of mind. My attention was given to something far more positive. At the outset of Youth Services International, Dixie asked me, "When is it going to be my turn?" About four years into the YSI venture, I turned the reins over to others and decided to at least try to start putting my deserving wife first. When YSI had its first public offering in 1993, I'd also made a lot of money, so I felt even more comfortable taking a few small steps toward that condition I'd always avoided — retirement.

Even though I spent much of my youth on the streets of Sioux City, farm life was the cornerstone of my principles and values, and these feelings were shared by Dixie who was a small-town girl at heart. In 1995 we bought Rich Meadow Farm, ninety-plus acres of rolling farm country in Westminster, Maryland, and began a chapter of our lives that looked toward "smelling the roses" rather than our usual attempt to cultivate them.

The farm had a history Dixie and I both appreciated. The original home on the property, built in the 1700s, was well preserved along with additions that were added in the eighteenth and nineteenth centuries. After we bought it, the centuries-old bank barn with walls of blue limestone was returned to its original beauty, and large stalls and brick walkways replaced the milk stalls and concrete walkways of the previous dairy farm operations. The milk house became a beautiful office area with screened porch and deck overlooking the one-and-a-half-acre fishing pond, which also provided a home for wild ducks and geese, and a pair of black swans.

With the restoration of the barn and other buildings on the property and my lifelong love of horses, it was only natural that Rich Meadow Farm would become a broodmare farm, breeding and raising horses. Since my earliest years at Grandpa Wharton's farm I've had an affinity for these majestic creatures and dreamed of owning my own horse farm.

Off to the Races

When I first contemplated entering the horse business, an old pro told me, "Jim, I gotta tell ya, this is a business where ninety percent of the participants lose money every year. You gotta set your goals high, but be prepared to lose, and to lose often. Who knows if you'll ever make any money, but Jim, there's just something inside of a horse that's good for a man. It's not gonna be about the money made or lost, it's going to be about the memories you make and the people you meet."

Sold! Of course I wanted to be involved. I loved farm life, I loved horses, and I was a gambling man at heart. You have to take risks if you want the rewards that life has to offer.

The horse business is indeed a game of risk — a high stakes poker game. It's a business comprised of hustlers, swindlers, and educated-guessers. You never know what you're getting, but you study, and study, and study until you get lucky with that one "big horse," the high-stakes winner. Then, boom, it's back in business, baby! That's the way it works and that's why I loved it.

I'd always had a sharp eye for talent. I used that ability to find and hire personnel that led my various endeavors to the top of the worlds of business and college athletics. In the fall of 1997, I decided I was going to put those evaluation skills to use again by purchasing young racing prospects as well.

I dreamt of the day when my homebred would trot the great track in Kentucky, roses draped around its neck and pride in its eyes. Spring was always filled with excitement as the new little foals were born, with the anticipation that anyone of them could become a winner. With the care and nurturing of the Rich Meadow team, a couple of our yearling foals sold for over a half million dollars at the yearling auctions in Kentucky, and we raised a horse that won almost a million dollars on the racetrack. I enjoyed not only the horses, but the challenges involved in the continual study and planning involved in the business — breeding plans, stallion selection, foal evaluations, and training programs for the young contenders. As they say, "A bad day at the track is better than…well, just about any other day."

All in all, Rich Meadow was my way of settling down, allowing me to examine my life and return to my roots. The horse business strengthened my relationship with not just my wife but my children and grandchildren, and led me to some of my closest friendships, while reawakening past relationships with people I cared for deeply. You might say this was retirement "Jim Hindman style."

Full Circle

Between 1993 and 1998 our family was blessed with the birth of four grandchildren, Kate and Kelly, Hannah and Eli. As they grew so did their love for the farm. They loved spending time on the farm, and Dixie and I loved having them. I taught them how to fish in our big pond and how to look for night-crawlers to bait the hook. We took walks in the rolling pastures and found birds' nests and groundhog holes together. I showed them our little foals and taught them how to approach a horse safely.

One day Eli and I were sitting at the end of the dock that extends over our little pond, casting fishing lines and passing the time. We didn't say much to each other, we just enjoyed the simple pleasures of fishing and being in each other's company. Finally, Eli broke the silence, "Grandpa, we're just like you and your grandfather!"

At that moment I realized that my life had come full circle and that I had succeeded in becoming the man I had always hoped to be. I had achieved affluence through the American free market, provided for my wife and children, and was now able to spend time with my beloved grandchildren on the farm I had always dreamed of owning. Surely at this moment I found the "something more" of life.

Back in the Saddle

Finding peace didn't necessarily mean that I could relax. In 1996 a friend told me about a business opportunity she thought I might be able to help with. She and three other small resellers of software used in engineering, architecture, facilities management, data management, and manufacturing were trying to form one larger company. Essentially the company would provide computer-aided design to those who needed it. She and her partners had contracted with the creators of the software to market it for them, and they saw tremendous growth potential.

94

The project appealed to me. I understood what they were trying to do, and could also see that they needed a broader view and approach. They were all trying to sell things individually and needed help to pull the diverse pieces together into a team. I figured I could easily fit this in with my equine adventures because it was mainly a matter of mentoring and guidance, at first at least. But, the company soon got into some trouble, and so I got heavily involved in the actual management and also brought in Scotty Walsh, a leader from IBM, and together we made Avatech Solutions a great success. Their services ultimately included the development of applications, data archiving, process optimization, technical support, and training, and their clients included not just businesses, but also government agencies and educational institutions around the world.

The Good Life

At the close of 1998, not only was I enjoying life on the farm and in the business world, but my eyesight, six years after the diagnosis, was still 20/20 with glasses. In fact, my vision was so unproblematic that I never even gave a second thought to my macular degeneration — it was as if I had never been diagnosed in the first place. All that was about to quickly change.

My dad, Staff Sergeant
Robert Ray Hindman,
in 1942, serving
his country in our war
against Fascism.

A beloved photo of
my father, and grandma
Cloie Alice Hindman

This is me in 1936,
looking forward to a happy,
eventful life.

Dixie in 1938.
"She must have been
a beautiful baby..."

"'...cause baby,
look at her now!"
The lovely Dixie,
a year before she
took my hand
in marriage in 1955.

My younger brothers
Tommy, Robert and me,
ready to take on
the world in 1950.

My graduation picture
from Central High School,
Sioux City, Iowa.

I loved being a Marine (me in 1954).
Once a Marine, always a Marine!

The luckiest day
in my life:
The day I married Dixie
(June 15, 1958)

Back to my
military
crew cut look.
(The kids I coached
started calling me
"Sir.")

Family!
The greatest loves
of my life –
Tim, Dixie and Cindi.

Dixie and
me in 1990.

Our 50th Wedding anniversary!
Thank you for your love and devotion, Dixie.

CHAPTER 13
SLIPPING INTO DARKNESS

Small Change, Big Challenge

Sometime in 1999 I began noticing a few small black spots in my vision. Even still, my yearly checkups confirmed that my vision, corrected by glasses, was still 20/20. The spots caused me some concern, but still not enough to do anything substantial to confront the enemy.

I did make one small change, though. I began to look at an Amsler Grid every so often. Basically a piece of graph paper with a dot in the center, I was told to look at the chart regularly, positioning it about arm's length from my face and taking turns with each eye to focus on the center dot. The warning sign was if I noticed that the lines were getting wavy or were in some other way obscured.

I kept the grid in my desk drawer and pulled it out once in a while to look at it. At first there was very little distortion in the grid, then one day the lines started to waver, and then suddenly the grid became a jumbled mess. That got my attention and I immediately made an appointment with Dr. Goldberg at the Johns Hopkins Wilmer Eye Institute.

Goldberg saw that the progression of macular degeneration was already negatively affecting my spirits. He also knew I was a risk-taker and so he mentioned a study being conducted by Wilmer on macular degeneration and asked if I would be interested in participating. I trusted him and had no fear of the unknown, so I agreed to participate.

This research project, The Complications of Age-Related Macular Degeneration Prevention Trial (CAPT), was meant to assess whether treating a certain contributing component of macular degeneration (drusen) with an infrared laser beam reduced the loss of vision or slowed the development of AMD. I received two of these laser treatments. The treatments didn't have any notable effect that I'm aware of and as quickly as I joined the study it ended. Whatever hope I might have briefly had, was gone.

Depressed and then Some

It was amazing how quickly things went south after that. Every time I mustered the courage to face the Amsler Grid I saw less of it. I quickly began to lose confidence and hope. The more distorted the grid became, the lower my heart and spirit sank. Wherever my vision was and wherever it was going to end up, I knew for sure that my future prospects weren't good.

When I was first diagnosed with AMD, I don't think anyone ever told me or showed me what the implications of the disease were — that my vision loss would be real, gradual, and steady. Maybe they did tell me, but it never really sunk in. But looking at that Amsler Grid, I came to know for sure the implications of the disease for myself. It was absolutely devastating. The world was growing dark right in front of me and there was nothing I could do about. I was losing hope.

Meanwhile, Back in the Real World

Thankfully, there were glimmers of hope shining out of from my past and present business successes. In 1999 I was named an Honorary Life Member of the International Franchise Association, the same organization that had honored me as the Entrepreneur of the Year in 1987 for my Jiffy Lube efforts. The release for this recognition stated, "Jim Hindman...has exhibited a unique combination of entrepreneurial spirit, leadership, and educational commitment throughout his varied career that included franchising, hospital management, coaching college football, mentoring troubled youth, and breeding thoroughbred horses." These were kind words, indeed, as well as some well-timed and much-needed encouragement.

Also, in 2000 and 2001, some of our horses, including Slew Valley (our homebred) and Dawn of the Condor, were beginning to win races, and this was a real thrill for me. If not for the macular degeneration, this might have been the height of my career and my life in general. Unfortunately, the macular degeneration was beginning to wreak some real havoc on my life, and the worst was yet to come.

Bad to Worse

As 2001 progressed, the vision in my right eye continued to deteriorate. Though by the official measurement it was still 20/25 with glasses, my eye's ability to function was severely diminished. Of course, it was equally frustrating to be looking through two eyes with different visual acuity. Navigating the world became increasingly difficult.

I continued to visit Dr. Goldberg regularly even though he told me that there was very little that could be done to stop the march of the disease. I began taking an Age-Related Eye Disease Study (AREDS) supplement formulation, the only treatment available, which is recommended for people with early AMD to slow the progress of the disease. He also suggested that I try glasses with yellow-tinted lenses to improve contrast and cut down on glare. In terms of a cure or some more substantial, if not permanent, treatment, Goldberg felt my only hope might be stem cell therapy. But that was still way off in the future, if it were ever to become a reality at all. So, I took my pills and wore my yellow shades and practically accepted the inevitable. "You've got macular degeneration and there's nothing you can do about it." Still, I wasn't about to give up and let AMD beat me. That was my plan anyway.

CHAPTER 14
THE BOTTOM'S GOTTA BE AROUND HERE SOMEWHERE

Getting the Better of Me

As the months and years passed, I did whatever I could to block out the reality of the progression of the macular degeneration. Basically, I just tried to keep on going, in spite of my ever-worsening vision. I did my best to not let on to anyone that my vision was in fact getting worse, making it more difficult for me to do average, everyday tasks. After a while, though, all the little things added up to one obvious conclusion — macular degeneration was getting the better of me.

Grounded!

Surrendering my driver's license was a monumental moment of despair. I was driving home one evening — and to that point I really had little trouble driving, especially during the day — and when I rounded a corner onto an unlit street everything went black. It wasn't just dark, it was a complete blackout. I was scared, not really for me but for other people. What if I hit someone, or killed a child? I knew a man who accidently hit and killed a child in his car, and he never got over it. I knew I had to get out of the driver's seat, and not just for the night, but for good. I could have refused to accept the fact that my vision was such that I shouldn't be driving, but I voluntarily gave up my license because I knew I had to.

Driving is a great privilege, though many people feel it is a right. It's certainly a rite of passage — when you're a teenager, you get your license. In South Dakota when I was growing up, you didn't need a license. Like many other youngsters, I was driving trucks and cars by the age of twelve. The loss of this ability, after more than sixty years behind the wheel, was completely demoralizing. I knew that from that point on I would have to rely on someone else to go anywhere. It was a complete loss of independence, and I didn't do well with dependency.

Sliding

As the years progressed so did the macular degeneration. The black spots steadily increased over the years, even while my vision remained fairly stable. All that changed drastically in 2004. The vision in my right eye dropped to 20/50, then to 20/200, and became even worse in 2005. My left eye, on the other hand, hung strong around 20/25. Together, however, my eyes were becoming increasingly useless.

It was all downhill from there. I looked, but didn't see. Everything blurred together and my field of view became a melting pot of foggy images and smears of color.

A World of Losses

It's impossible to recount all of the things I lost because of my increasing blindness. I kept trying to overcome my limitations, until I finally realized that I was going to have to do something I never did before — give up. It isn't that I gave up hope, but I was forced to give up participating in activities I really loved. That is probably the hardest thing to deal with: coming to grips with giving up. It just wasn't in my nature and I was reluctant every step of the way.

What's the Point?

As my vision deteriorated, activities became more and more

difficult and so I found myself withdrawing from them and from others. I gave up reading the newspaper and following sports. It was one thing to stop watching basketball, baseball, and football games on television, but quite another to give up watching our grandkids' games. I still went at times to be part of the crowd, but it wasn't the same. One of my great pleasures as a grandfather was watching our grandchildren play their sports and participate in their other activities. Now, attending these events was little more than a bitter reminder of everything I had lost and was continuing to lose. I literally missed out on years of their young lives.

I also withdrew from my social life more generally. I didn't want to go anywhere for two reasons. First, I didn't want to go because I really couldn't see anything and so I felt I couldn't participate in or otherwise enjoy whatever was going on. Second, I didn't want to embarrass myself.

Some time ago, I traveled to New York to visit my old friend George Lois. We met at a restaurant, always a challenging environment because of the commotion and the typical low lighting. Anyway, I was eager to catch up with him and reserved no passion in giving him a hearty bear hug. I don't know who was more surprised, George or the man I was hugging! Apparently I had spotted the wrong man, and, thinking he was my good buddy, embraced him instead of George. If it weren't so funny it would have been completely embarrassing. Nevertheless, it was a shot to my pride and ego — being unable to even recognize my own friend.

Before the macular degeneration really set in, I had a very busy schedule and was active in a number of areas in community life. I was involved in politics, volunteer programs, athletics, fundraising, and helping to orchestrate local events. I served on the board of directors of Morningside College and the Baltimore

Symphony Orchestra. I went to plays and concerts, club meetings, luncheons, banquets, and other social events. Unable to see, however, I gave it all up.

At first family and friends insisted I go wherever it was with them. Eventually, though, they stopped asking. I said "no" enough times, they got the point. So, the more I withdrew the more others withdrew from me. Essentially I gave up my whole social network, and, in turn, I guess they gave up on me. I withdrew to the point that I didn't really care to go anywhere, ever. I was pretty much satisfied to sit home and listen to a book — a far cry from my former life.

From Jetsetter to Homebody

In my highflying business days, I was constantly traveling. During the Jiffy Lube and YSI years we had a corporate jet, so jaunts across the state or country were common. I always enjoyed the trips, whether they were to a convention or to meet with other business leaders or government officials. When I worked for TWA, I had an unlimited flight pass, guaranteeing me a seat at all times, and among other places, I flew back and forth often between Orlando and TWA headquarters in Kansas City. I traveled on the Concorde across the Atlantic more than once, for negotiations in France.

The horse business, too, meant trips to Kentucky and other places to check out promising yearlings. As a coach I traveled up and down the South and East and Midwest, scouting for talent of a different kind.

To relax, I'd go to the Black Hills or other places in the Wild West for vacations, or join groups of friends or business associates for river cruises in Europe. I'd been able to visit and enjoy many of the greatest places in this country and the world. I often went to the big games, too — the World Series, the NBA Finals, and the Super Bowl. If I saw something I wanted to do, I made it happen.

And whether I traveled for business or pleasure, whether I was in Ireland, Australia, Iceland, or Paris, I always immersed myself in the environment and atmosphere of a place and its people. The opportunity to take in all of the sights, sounds, and smells of new and different places was a joy of my life.

I gave all of this up as my eyesight worsened. It was frustrating to not be in control anymore, to have to rely on others when traveling. But even more, it was completely disheartening to not be able to enjoy the scenery of some new or even familiar locale. I travelled to have new adventures, to see new things. That was no longer possible, so I stopped.

How to Fail in Business Without Even Trying

As an executive in the world of business, it was not my job to do something but to make sure that it got done. In this position, one of my primary responsibilities was reading reports. My success depended on my ability to take in information and connect the dots toward innovative results in a timely manner. As I've said, knowledge is power. But, macular degeneration made it impossible for me to read as I once did; and, unable to read I couldn't offer much by way of advice, input, or direction. I was losing my ability to contribute. I was losing purpose.

If an inability to read reports caused me to lose effectiveness, the inability to read faces did twofold. I used to be able to read a face. I believed what people were saying — or not — by noting the way they looked when they delivered any news, report, or their position on a policy. Being able to recognize subtle changes in expression, such as signs of fear, pride, doubt, or hesitancy — all of those things were critical in the course of regular business. With macular degeneration, however, all of those clues were lost to me. Unable to make that all-important eye contact when talking to someone, I gave up the edge in my business dealings. I never would have imagined how much those little, almost imperceptible, gestures added to the context of conversations and interactions. But, once that ability to gauge a person through their expression was lost because of my worsening vision, I realized just how valuable sight was in nearly everything I did.

Mounting frustration over the fact that I could hardly read anything led me to withdraw from business. I resigned from the board of Avatech, thinking it was better if I just got out of the way.

Lost in the Crowd

More frustrating than my inability to be effective in the business world — Avatech was just a little side project to me, to keep me occupied — were the challenges I faced in operating my beloved horse business. Evaluating the new foals, a potential horse for our racing stable, or a new broodmare at the auctions, studying the stallion guides for matches with the mares, reading reports, and even identifying my own horses at the racetrack, eventually all these things became almost impossible.

Losing my eyesight was robbing me of not only pleasure and satisfaction, but of pride. At the racetrack, with all the sights, the colors, the action, I could never seem to find and keep my focus on our horse. He would trot into the saddle area, and just when I thought I had him in my sights, I would lose him. The time I asked my friends where our horse was, and they, thinking I was joking, said, "Right there," pointing about ten feet in front of us, I knew it was time to give up yet another thing I loved so dearly.

Not only did I decide to get out the business, I also gave up watching the races entirely. What was the point of going to the track when I couldn't see the races anyway? It wasn't very much fun to watch a race when I couldn't follow the horses around the track. One by one, the loss of vision due to macular degeneration forced me out of the activities I enjoyed most. Having given up so much, I was scared to consider what I might lose next.

Lights Out

Years passed from the day I turned in my driver's license, and while I didn't particularly like it, I grew accustomed to having someone else drive me wherever I needed to go. I considered what an imposition it must have been on others, but no one seemed to mind. A former player and employee, Dave Dolch, whom I also coached football with for a few years at Bowie State during my YSI years, was often generous enough, when he was in the area, to drive me around. Of course, everyone knew that the macular degeneration was giving me trouble, but I did whatever I could to hide the extent to which I was being affected.

After running around to a few places and having some dinner, Dave drove me home and let me out in front of my garage, just as he had countless times before. He pulled away and I was set to make the short, fifty or so foot walk to the front door. But, when he rounded the circular driveway I lost the benefit of the illumination from his car's headlights. The sudden change from the brightness of the headlights to the dark of the night made me pause in my tracks as I waited for my eyes to adjust. They didn't. I waited a minute or two but nothing changed. I couldn't see a thing. I couldn't even see the hand in front of my own face.

I carefully shuffled my feet towards the garage door, arms outstretched in front of me to avoid running into anything. Finally, I felt the door and began groping around in the hopes of localizing my position. If I could make my way to the side, I figured, I could then easily locate the walking path, and from there hopefully make my way to the door. I found the edge of the garage door, but still couldn't make out the path. I didn't want to do anything stupid, to try to make my way to the door in the pitch black and trip over something and hurt myself. So, I didn't move.

What a night! There I was, outside my own house, in my own driveway, no more than fifty feet from my own front door, and I was basically stuck.

As a young child on the streets of Sioux City, I was tough as nails. Nothing scared me. And yet, here I was, a grown man, having overcome every obstacle that life had imposed, and now I was trapped outside my own home.

Defeated, I grabbed my cellphone and called into the house to ask Dixie to come get me. Talk about a shot to my pride!

At that moment I realized that I had to do something serious about this macular degeneration, and I needed to do it quickly. If I was going to maintain any level of functional sight, any semblance of a quality life, I was going to have to find a way out of this darkness.

CHAPTER 15
THE SEARCH

Game Plan

The installation of a motion-sensor spotlight above the garage door was a good first step in helping me deal with my vision loss, but I knew that if I was going to beat macular degeneration I needed something more than a simple light. But I didn't know how to battle this enemy, the biggest problem being that the enemy was me. It was my own eyes that were causing me such problems, my own physical limitations that I could not beat.

Initially I thought that going to the best eye hospital in the country was the best I could do. And no doubt, I received invaluable assistance from the folks at Wilmer. Still, I wasn't content to do nothing. So I visited other hospitals, hoping for some other prognosis. Maybe they knew about some revolutionary treatment for AMD that could help me. Unfortunately, everywhere I went the professionals confirmed what I'd already been told, **"You're going blind and there's nothing you can do about it."** Regardless of what anyone — what everyone — told me, I kept searching. The more people told me there was nothing that could be done, the surer I was that I would eventually find something I could do.

At some point in my rather chaotic search I ended up at a clinic somewhere near the Florida Everglades. I saw an ad that said they were treating macular degeneration patients with some new therapy and so I knew I had to check it out. Turning off a major highway, we followed a gravel road for miles through the marshes until we finally came upon a dilapidated building in the middle of nowhere. It might have been the buoys and life-preservers adorning the walls, but whatever it was, we pulled out of the parking lot as quickly as we pulled in. I don't know if the guy was a witchdoctor or a board certified practitioner, but I knew enough that whoever he was, if they couldn't treat me at Wilmer he couldn't either.

It was clear, if I was going to really beat this thing, I needed a plan. I needed to set out my objectives and then devise a scheme to accomplish them. Plan, organize, control: that was my motto in business and in coaching, and I was about to implement this strategy in my battle against AMD.

Doing Something Now

Obviously, my ultimate goal was — and still is — to find a total cure for this disease, to get 100% of my vision back. But I realized that if a cure was out there, it was still some way off. I needed to do something immediately to help me retain whatever vision I could and to make the most of whatever vision I still had. I had never heard of low vision rehabilitation, so the best I could think to do was make my life easier through the use of assistive equipment. If the garage light worked I was sure I could find other helpful devices.

Dr. Magoo!

Throughout my battle with AMD Mr. Magoo has been something of an inspiration for me. Despite his obvious visual impairment he always managed to make it through the day, and unscathed at that. If ever there was a prospective spokesperson for macular degeneration, Dr. Magoo, as I affectionately call him, would be it.

At any rate, I never wore glasses before I had AMD, but eventually I gave in and tried some with heavy frames and very thick, Magoo-type lenses. I wore them for less than a year. They were just too bulky, heavy, and uncomfortable. They also made it all too clear to everyone around me that I had a vision problem. Call it vanity, but I just didn't want everyone to be looking at me like I was some sort of charity-case, like I was someone in need of other people's sympathy. Overall, glasses helped, but the Magoo-lenses were out.

Reading was one of the first activities macular degeneration gave me problems with. With some effort I could read large-print books and magazines, but even then reading was a struggle. The glasses only helped so much. So, I researched and found some devices that could help make reading easier and more enjoyable. I purchased two machines: one that actually reads the text out loud to me, and another that projects an enlarged image of whatever it is I want to read onto a color screen. For years I struggled to read on my own, but with these devices I was able to enjoy again an activity that brought me so much pleasure.

Apart from those more expensive devices, I began to rely on a trusty 99¢ hand-held magnifying glass. I put one on a lanyard, a helpful tip from my friend and fellow IMT™ patient Tom Sarver, and I never leave home without it. When reading menus or labels in a grocery store, the magnifier is worth every penny!

Even with all these fixes, I was still somewhat dissatisfied. They did make my life easier and more enjoyable, and I felt more connected and useful because I was again participating in activities I really enjoyed. Still, these devices were only partial solutions. They were necessary and helpful, but they weren't the big prize — the cure.

Never, Never Give Up

A high school classmate and lifelong friend once told me that my most remarkable attribute was my determination. Whether climbing ropes faster than anyone else in gym class, training harder and preparing longer for a football game, or taking on a business venture, whatever I did, I did it with determination. This was the same kind of steely resolve I needed to take on AMD.

Of course, the impositions posed by this disease forced me to change how I lived. I had to give up activities, give up control, let others help me more often, and compensate in other ways for my declining vision. But, over time I found that the biggest obstacle to my living well despite the macular degeneration, was my own outlook. Initially I guess I felt sorry for myself, but once I determined to get past my own self-imposed mental barriers my disposition changed for the better. I was sure I wasn't the only person hoping for a cure to this disease, and so I believed that somebody out there must be working on a solution, something that would help. And, even if it was experimental, I was going to find it and get in on it.

CHAPTER 16
THE SOLUTION

At My Fingertips

I continued to pursue any and all medical breakthroughs for the treatment of AMD. My persistent search led me to visit specialists all across the United States. After learning of a new procedure that could supposedly restore some degree of sight for macular degeneration sufferers, I was ready to travel to Europe, the only place I was aware it was available, to explore how I could take advantage of this new technology. The device, as far as I understood it, was a tiny telescope that, incredibly, was implanted right into the eye of AMD patients. The telescope projected an enlarged image onto the retina, thus compensating somewhat for the loss of visual acuity caused by the degeneration of the macula. The operation was already being successfully done in Europe and there was a team in the U.S. evaluating people for it.

A few phone calls later and I was on a train to New York to meet with the team, fingers crossed that I might even get the device right then and there. The doctors examined me for the procedure, then delivered the bad news — **I didn't qualify**.

Apparently, although it was approved in Europe, the manufacturer was still seeking FDA approval in the U.S. For that, they needed to select patients who they believed would respond especially well to the implantation of the telescope in order to report the best possible results. According to their diagnosis, I did not qualify because the defect in my retina created by the damaged macula was too large. The doctors also didn't think the implant would improve my vision sufficiently to warrant the surgery.

Although I understood their concerns, disappointment clouded my thoughts and weighted my footsteps as I left the office and boarded the Metro for the return trip to Baltimore. I was so close to getting some of my vision back, but now I really had to consider if my sight was gone for good. My optimism was yet again waning.

Doing My Homework

Still, I couldn't give up all hope. I knew that there was something out there that could restore some of my lost vision, and so I went to work finding out everything I could about the amazing device.

I loved the fact that an entrepreneur like myself had a hand in the making of the implantable miniature telescope, the IMT™, as it is called. Making conversation during a routine consultation, an ophthalmologist described an idea he had for helping patients suffering from end-stage AMD by implanting a very small telescope in their eye. But, it was only an idea. However, the patient was inspired by the idea, and, as an entrepreneur, set out exploring the possibility of creating an intraocular device that could help macular degeneration sufferers regain some vision. His research eventually led to the implantable miniature telescope. And, once it was determined that the device did in fact help patients, Vision-Care Ophthalmic Technologies was established by Yossi Gross and Dr. Isaac Lipshitz.

The technology used in the telescope is so miniaturized it is almost in the realm of nanotechnology. The use of three air bubbles in the design of the optical portion of the device resulted in a telescope that produces a magnification of very close to 3x for a device that is only 3.6mm in diameter and 4.4mm in length.

"The development process was not a simple one, and the manufacturing process was even more challenging; requiring the development of special processes and unique machinery," says VisionCare. "The first version of the device did not produce the desired improvement in visual acuity, so the development team returned to the drawing board. They came back with a better design that resulted in improved performance and provided a wider field of vision."

The IMT™ is not a cure, but a device to help people use their remaining vision better. It magnifies the overall image one is looking at while reducing the relative size of the central blind spot caused by macular degeneration. By magnifying the central visual field using two to three times magnification on the macular area, the image falls on a larger area and the patient is able to use enough photoreceptor cells to create an image that can be detected by the brain.

Again, it is not a panacea. "It's important that patients know that this device is not going to allow them to drive," says Dr. Oliver D. Schein, a professor of ophthalmology at the Wilmer Eye Institute. "It's not going to let them read small print. But it may take someone who has had to give up reading entirely and get them to the point where they can read large print." As Dr. Judith Goldstein, chief of Wilmer's Low Vision and Vision Rehabilitation department, notes, "This doesn't make the macular degeneration go away...and it doesn't mean you won't still need visually assistive devices." Realistic goals, she explains, include improving the overall clarity of distance vision, being able to see people's faces and expressions, and being able to view bright colors and images in more detail.

Realistic goals for sight after an IMT implant:
Recognizing faces of family and friends
Watching TV
Reading
Hobbies like painting, knitting, **Unrealistic goals:**
or gardening
Driving
Seeing a golf ball in flight
Playing tennis
Never having to use a magnifying glass again

An FDA study found that nine out of ten patients with the telescope implant experienced improved vision by at least two lines on the eye chart. And some patients did even better than that. The distributor of the IMT™, CentraSight, notes that, "In a survey conducted during the FDA clinical trial, patients who received the telescope implant generally reported that they were less dependent on others, less frustrated and worried about their vision, less limited in their ability to see, and better able to visit with others and recognize facial expressions. Overall, the survey findings showed patients had a clinically important improvement in quality of life." The report on the one-year results of the IMT™ trial surgeries noted that IMT™ implant patients had an improved ability to do both "static and dynamic tasks at distance, intermediate, and near ranges." One possible explanation for this is that the device enables patients to use natural eye movements to see both near and far, and it is not something they have to hold or manipulate.

A number of considerations enter into the doctors' evaluation of whether someone is a good candidate for an IMT™ implant. Something that rules out many people is previous cataract surgery, which a high percentage of older people have undergone. Due to surgical risks, a patient must have at least one eye with AMD that has not had cataract surgery to be able to receive an IMT™ implantation. A patient must also have central blindness in both eyes that is uncorrectable by eyeglasses, contact lenses, medication, or other eye surgery.

Attitude and temperament count, too. When the Emory Eye Center in Atlanta evaluates potential candidates, for example, they look for people who are optimistic, highly motivated, and able to accept compromises. Rehabilitation takes considerable effort and motivation, so any candidate should be mentally and physically prepared to push through frustrations and difficulties along the way.

No surgery is risk-free, and the IMT™ is no exception. The risks in this case include many of the same adverse effects that can once in a great while result from cataract surgery, including inflammation or raised pressure in the eye after surgery, swelling of the cornea, and other cornea issues. It is also possible for inflammatory deposits to develop on the device itself, and as the manufacturer of the IMT™ points out, "Individual results may vary. There is a risk that having this surgery could worsen your vision rather than improve it."

Apart from chance complications, when the IMT™ is implanted, it disrupts the peripheral vision in that eye. What this means in practical terms is that the eye with the IMT™ will need to be trained to focus on central images only, while the other, non-implanted eye, with whatever degradation of sight it may have due to macular degeneration, will be used for obtaining peripheral images. Further, since the two eyes are now quite different — one seeing close and central images, the other only peripheral images — accurate depth perception will be diminished. The American Academy of Ophthalmology points out another thing to be aware of, "Contrast sensitivity is reduced in macular degeneration in general, and the telescope probably diminishes it even more." And once the device is in place, it is more difficult for doctors to see and evaluate the macula, which still must be continually monitored for further progression of macular degeneration.

A Second Look

So, I did my homework, weighed the risks and rewards, and decided that if I could, I still desperately wanted to get the device. After all, the choice was essentially between doing nothing and definitely not gaining any level of vision, and doing something and more than likely getting some vision back. I was certain I wanted to get the device, but I had already been told I couldn't. So, I moved on. I didn't forget about the IMT™ or the promise it held for me, but I went in search of something else that could help me immediately.

Stem cell therapies again caught my attention. But I realized that despite their promise, that was an answer even farther off than the IMT™. I considered other magnification devices, but it seemed absurd to me to have to wear or carry around some oversized piece of equipment. Besides, I had been down that road before, and it didn't work for me.

A Second Chance

One of my great blessings throughout life has been a large circle of friends and close relationships. Many of these friendships have continued for decades, and no matter where life's journey has taken each of us, we've always stayed in touch.

In September 2012, my longtime friend Gil Campbell called from Florida to share an article that had appeared recently in the Daytona Beach *News-Journal*. His son Mike had played football for me at Western Maryland, and Gil and I had also been partners in Jiffy Lube. The account he called to my attention described the successful implant of a miniature telescope in the eye of a patient with macular degeneration, resulting in the successful restoration of sight by physicians at the University of California, Davis. This was the same tiny telescope I'd heard about and investigated much earlier, when it was still in experimental stages. The device helped many patients see two to four lines better on the eye test chart, and improved their ability to do everyday tasks such as reading, watching TV, and recognizing faces.

I tracked down the article immediately, and wrote a letter to the University of California, Davis. If they would have me, I was going to head across the country for the surgery. Thank goodness I had the sense to copy my good friend at Johns Hopkins Wilmer Eye Institute, Dr. Morton Goldberg.

Dr. Goldberg responded right away, stating that extensive research and clinical trials, including some at Wilmer, had been conducted on the Implantable Miniature Telescope in the past few years. In 2010, it had received FDA approval for patients over age seventy-five who had end-stage AMD and met certain other criteria. The cost of the device, approximately $15,000 (not including the surgery itself or rehabilitation), was also fully covered by Medicare. He went on to say that after evaluation, I could possibly qualify as a candidate for the IMT™ surgery, in which case I would be the first patient to receive the IMT™ at Wilmer since FDA approval had been granted.

By the time our conversation came to a close, my spirits were soaring. Dr. Goldberg's invitation couldn't have been more welcome.

Testing and Qualifying

With a mix of enthusiasm and trepidation, I, again, took the next step to see if I was indeed a viable candidate for the IMT™. Over the next few weeks, I had several examinations with Wilmer's Low Vision and Vision Rehabilitation Service teams, including occupational therapists, and with Oliver Schein, M.D., the Burton E. Grossman Professor of Ophthalmology, who would perform the surgery if it was approved. Dr. Schein had been involved in testing the device for years in the clinical trials, making him Wilmer's expert in this technology.

It was determined that I was indeed a suitable candidate for the IMT™ because my present vision (or lack thereof) fit the criteria, I had never had cataract surgery, and when Dr. Goldstein tested me with a simulator, my vision improved tremendously. This simulator was nothing fancy, just a little handheld telescope that enabled a person to see what their vision could be like after IMT™ surgery.

Picture Perfect

The day I tried it out they just handed me the simulator, told me to put it up to my eye, and asked my wife Dixie, who had accompanied me, to go down to the end of the hall, about twenty yards away. It was amazing, I could see her as clear as day — a sight I hadn't seen in years. And what a perfect image to welcome me back into the world of sight! Until that moment I never realized just how much I lost because of macular degeneration. The impact was profound. Right then I was convinced that the IMT™ was for me and I couldn't wait to have the operation.

Not so Fast

The team at Wilmer went on to explain the details of the implant itself, how it worked, and what kind of results I could expect from it. The discussions that followed with family and friends about the IMT™ resulted in both positive and negative responses. One in particular sticks in my mind: Did I really want to be the first patient at Wilmer to get the device? First in line was exactly where I wanted to be! It was reminiscent of my early school days and time at the Boys and Girls Home. No matter what it was — recess, school dismissal, or the chow line — I was going to be first. The IMT™ surgery would be no different!

Gratitude

Once I found out I could get the operation done at Wilmer, I asked to see their development officer. I told him I had once planned to go to Europe for this operation and would probably have paid all of that out of pocket. Thus, I was willing to make a contribution to some project of theirs — this would be the easiest grant they ever got. I ended up donating $50,000 to the Arnall Patz endowed professorship for the Lions Vision Center, which was a perfect fit. Dr. Patz, 2006 recipient of the Lions Clubs International Foundation Humanitarian Award, was best known for his research in the late 1940s into the cause of blindness for many premature infants. He had hypothesized that the infants were receiving too much oxygen, but he received no support and was even told to not pursue his intuitions. He ignored the command and was later proved to be right, thus saving the sight of countless babies then and since. He also developed one of the first laser instruments for the treatment of retinal blood vessel diseases. The person serving as the Arnall Patz professor would concentrate on the development of better equipment for those with low vision, further research in the field, and the recruitment of additional personnel to better serve the low vision community.

Surgery Day: "You're so Brave!"

On December 3, 2012, twenty years after my initial diagnosis, I was at Wilmer to have the IMT™ surgery. A simple outpatient procedure, they told me I would be home before lunch. Although I felt slightly uneasy about it, the professionals at Wilmer decided it best to have the IMT™ implanted in my left eye, which was actually my better seeing eye. It gave me pause to risk my stronger eye. But I made up my mind that Wilmer was in charge and I would follow their recommendation.

Really, once I signed on for the operation, I had no apprehensions at all. I had faith in the team and in what they said would happen. I also had confidence in Dr. Schein. So I didn't have any doubts about the outcome of the surgery, although I was a little uneasy, as many people are, about the idea of undergoing an operation on my eye while I was awake. I wanted to be put to sleep, but the operation is performed with local anesthesia.

As advertised, the surgery was quick, painless, and not in any way unpleasant. Perhaps a half-hour after receiving a dose of preanesthesia intravenously, I was given some numbing drops in my eye and wheeled into the operating room. I still felt completely at ease going into the surgery; although I do remember one of the nurses saying to me beforehand, "You are so brave." Frankly, that is the *last* thing you want to hear before undergoing surgery! But everything went well. The surgery lasted just forty-five minutes, and I was home soon thereafter. A swath of gauze over my eye, it would be a day or two before I could tell if the surgery was a success or not.

CHAPTER 17
WINDOW ON THE WORLD

A New World

I was eager to take the gauze off my eye, to start using my new telescope, and to begin exploring the world once again. So, early the next morning, with Dixie's help, I did the deed. Off came the bandage as I prepared to immediately see the world again for the first time. Unfortunately, my highest hopes were not quite met. "Is that it?" I thought to myself. The images I had seen with the simulator were much better than what I was seeing. My expectations and dreams, maybe they didn't come crashing to the ground, but they certainly came back to earth. To get the most out of the telescope, to get more completely back into the world of sight, was going to take more effort than I hoped.

Recovery

Overall, the initial recovery from the surgery was uneventful. My eye was swollen in the days that followed, and for what seemed like the better part of the first year. I was amazed at the difference between the two eyes right after the operation — the non-implanted eye felt normal, but the telescopic eye seemed enlarged. This also caused a feeling of pressure in my eye for a while. The swelling never really slowed me down, though, and the IMT™ eye eventually returned to feeling normal.

Since the IMT™ is sutured into place, I was told to be very careful following the procedure. I wore a protective eye patch for a few days and avoided all physical exertion, like lifting anything even remotely heavy, which might cause undue pressure in my eye. Whenever I went anywhere, I wore protective glasses rather than the eye patch, though the eye patch would certainly do the trick. Other than that, I just administered a few kinds of eye drops for a few weeks. One thing I was not prepared for was the constant tearing in my IMT™ eye. It was an odd sensation which also blurred my vision. This experience was as strange as it was frustrating, but it subsided after a few weeks.

I was expecting to experience some mild discomfort and a period of acclimation after the surgery, so I took those little surprises and adjustments in stride. However, what I didn't handle well was the lack of progress I was having with my vision through the IMT™. I wanted results, and I wanted them right away!

There were times in the days following surgery that I could see some things briefly and rather unclearly through my telescope, and there were other times when I couldn't see anything at all. On measure, my vision was actually worse right after the surgery than it was before. One reason for this was that most times when I could actually get the telescope to focus on an object I would begin seeing double. I often saw an image within an image. It was as if I was looking at something on a large TV screen and that exact image, only smaller, appeared within the larger picture. It was like when you're watching the news and also trying to follow the football game in a smaller box on your big screen — except that in my new eye, both the big screen and the small box were set to the same channel! For a few days right after the operation I couldn't help but wonder if this miracle device was ever going to work right for me.

V for Victory

Immediately after the surgery I had several doctor's appointments to make sure everything was healing properly and that I was progressing well. I sat in my ophthalmologist's screening room during my first follow-up visit ready to begin the all-too-familiar eye exam where I was told to identify letters I could not make out on an eye chart I could not really see. I was prepared to see just what I had grown accustomed to seeing — nothing! And, at first, that is precisely what I did see. But then, as I continued to stare at the chart, I suddenly realized that I could actually see some of the letters on that chart. The first letter I saw was a "V." "V," I thought to myself, is for Victory!

Nearly two decades of hoping, praying, and searching for something that would restore my vision — and I had finally found it. I could see again. It was amazing!

Never-Ending Practice

Before surgery my vision was 20/400, and that has improved to 20/60 in my IMT™ eye. That is just amazing! But, the key to such improvement is practice. The recovery process is simple enough, the rehabilitation process is more complicated, or at least takes more effort.

Shortly after my implant operation, as soon as the eye began to heal, Wilmer's Low Vision and Vision Rehabilitation Services guided and directed me through a post-surgery recovery program of "optical therapy." At first, it meant adjusting to the IMT™ with a black patch over the fellow eye (the eye without the lens transplant) as I did things like read or watch TV, then walking or moving from room to room without the patch, being careful to avoid losing my balance or falling. I also had to focus on various charts consisting of numbers, the alphabet, alphabet letters enclosed in blocks of progressive sizes, and others. I did these exercise for about two hours each day. The reason behind these rather mundane-but-necessary drills is to train the brain to use the IMT™ at will — that's the challenge.

With the challenges of practice and retraining the brain to properly work with the IMT™ what is needed most is a positive, determined mental attitude. Learning to switch smoothly between long-range and short-range vision was not a cinch, it required time and commitment — commitment to practice, practice, practice.

It Only Gets Better

It wasn't instantaneous, but the improvement was impressive. Before long I could see things that I'd given up trying to see. I could navigate my world again, and the IMT™ brought many things that were important to me back into focus.

When I first realized that macular degeneration was stealing my eyesight, and when I started giving up things to compensate for my worsening vision, I virtually resigned myself to a life of help-lessness and hopelessness. The exact opposite started happening with the IMT™. Every small success made me bolder, brought back new possibilities, and gave me the hope I needed to try new activities and reengage old ones. In short, the IMT™ not only gave me back my vision, it gave me back my purpose.

CHAPTER 18
RENEWED PURPOSE

Master of My Destiny

I've always said, "Everyone needs a purpose." A strong and clear purpose is the key to a good, long life. When I started to really lose my vision, I felt as though I no longer had any purpose, and so I gave up doing many things. I lost about ten years of vibrant life because I believed the lie that without full vision I could not live a meaningful life. The IMT™ helped me to see again, and restored a sense of purpose. I realize now, however, that there was no reason for me to give up so much.

Recently, I read a book called *The Encyclopedia of Sports and Recreation for People with Visual Impairments*, by Andrew Leibs. I was amazed — and inspired. The things people accomplish despite the loss or diminishing of vision is astounding. Reading these stories of inspiration made me realize more fully how much the potential we have within us can be developed. Blind athletes drive racecars, shoot archery, play darts, bowl, play baseball, ski, and climb mountains. There is very little a visually impaired person cannot do with enough motivation, accommodation, and imagination.

The biggest mistake I made, then, was not more proactively confronting macular degeneration. I had never heard of low vision rehabilitation — skills and devices designed to make living with low vision easier — and so I didn't take advantage of it. I didn't know about simple tips and tricks that could have made my life easier and more enjoyable. Mostly, I thought that once I lost my vision, that was it — I was useless, incapable, and without purpose. Yes, the IMT™ helped restore my passion for and purpose in life, but I bet I would never have lost it in the first place if I better understood the enemy I was battling and the techniques available to beat it.

Today, I am back as the master of my destiny. I believe it is my mind and my commitment to staying positive and impassioned that has most improved my life. Of course, it doesn't hurt that I can see again! But ultimately, I decide if I am going to get out of bed in the morning, and for what purpose. Each and every day I commit myself to maximizing my benefit to others. This is my purpose in life.

Giving Back

From childhood I've always had a strong desire to pay back what I consider to be my debt to society. Had it not been for a long line of great teachers, coaches, and colleagues, caring people and their generosity, I certainly would not be where I am today.

Financial success has provided me many opportunities to return my debt of gratitude. Through the years we gave to a number of great causes, including the establishment of a professorship at Harvard University and to the athletic program at Western Maryland College. Two other causes were even closer to my heart.

In 1989, in repayment to the great teachers and coaches Dixie and I had at Morningside College, we funded the creation of a new athletic facility, the largest single gift to that point ever to Morningside College. The result was a 71,000-square-foot building of modern design and state-of-the art equipment that included, among many other things, an elevated jogging track, weight room, sauna, three basketball courts, sun deck, and six-lane swimming pool with diving well. I wanted them to call this the Great Teachers and Coaches Facility, but the college insisted on giving us credit.

So, it ended up being called the Hindman-Hobbs Health, Physical Education, and Recreation Center, because my wife had been a student there too, and her parents helped me get started and gave me a wonderful wife. If the college was determined to name something after me, their name had to be on it too. The plaque in the front of the building lists the teachers and coaches who were influential in both Dixie's and my life. All of this was our effort to highlight their memories and talents for current and future students at our beloved alma mater.

I identify strongly with the Marines, and my time in the Marine Reserve was time I cherished. The Corps' focus on the development of citizenship and character, strength and discipline really resonated with me, and it did much to stretch my mental and physical boundaries. Thus, when a national museum of the Marine Corps hit the planning board in 2002, I wanted in on it. Located on a 135-acre site next to the Marine Corps base in Quantico, Virginia, the museum is a tribute to Marines past and present. I'm proud to be a part of the founders' group of the National Museum of the Marine Corps, created to preserve the memory of America's countless heroes and the many sacrifices they made for our freedom.

The Hindman Foundation

Donating money to great causes was but a small way of giving back to society. With the establishment of the Hindman Foundation many years ago, these types of efforts continue, but today I am interested in much more hands-on efforts.

After my years of effort to avoid blindness, and the miraculous restoration of some of my sight, I am driven and committed to do whatever possible to increase awareness of AMD — what people can do to fight it and live better with it. The IMT™ was the solution that worked for me, but it won't be the same for everyone. However, low vision rehabilitation and assistive services are generally helpful to anyone with low vision. Hopefully, this book will be a starting point for those experiencing AMD or low vision to search out what options exist for them.

The focus of the Foundation up to now has been primarily directed towards education. However, with the future funding of the Foundation, through the sale of this book and other efforts, it is my desire that this will become my legacy. Therefore, 100% of net proceeds from the publication of this book will be given to the Lions Clubs International Foundation (LCIF), Wills Eye Hospital in Philadelphia, and Wilmer Eye Institute at Johns Hopkins in Baltimore. Through these agencies, leaders in the fight against AMD and other eye-related diseases and malfunctions, the three critical elements of beating this disease will be met: education, rehabilitation, and research.

Returning to My Passions

I realize now that I will never retire. My work now is primarily mental, such as planning. The guy responsible for the show, me, mainly thinks about the big picture. When I am planning something, I usually visualize it in my mind and then share it with the troops. Then I delegate much of the execution to others with more specialized knowledge. I rely on my vision aids for anything I need to read. I've been an executive so long that I can think, but can't do much else. My job for a long time — long before AMD — has been seeing that things get done rather than doing them.

The clipboard and whistle are even back in my life. A young man who played for me at Western Maryland College, now Mc-Daniel, and was a partner in Jiffy Lube, Steve Luette, is now a very successful head football coach at a local high school. He had me give inspirational talks to his teams from time to time in recent years, and then he asked if I would consider coming down to help coach the team. "Any time you are available, we would love to have you."

Since I'd recovered from many of my AMD limitations, I really wanted to do this, but I pondered whether I would be able to commit the time to it, while I was kicking off my campaign to increase awareness of AMD. And could I trust my vision just yet? I certainly could still teach young men the thrill of the game, and the importance of growing physically, mentally, and spiritually. I might not be able to see everything, but I could surely see things such as footwork, and whether or not a player had his mind in the game, as well as serve as an ombudsman on tricky calls.

I finally decided to do it, and I'm loving every minute of it. Everyone around me has noted that I suddenly seem to have the old spring in my step and take-charge tone in my voice again.

And this is what it is really all about — not giving up control to AMD. Sure, there will be frustrations, setbacks, adjustments that need to be made, but in the end, it's all about attitude. You have to ask yourself this question: Am I going to give up all the things I love because I have macular degeneration, or am I going to do everything possible to keep doing everything I love despite the macular degeneration?

"Win or lose, there's nothing more thrilling in my life now than to be able to actually *see* one of my thoroughbreds run like the wind."

CHAPTER 19
YOUR CHALLENGE

The people whose lives we touch, our contributions to our country, our communities, and families, our faith in God and our fellow man, and what we strive to achieve, like stones tossed into a pond, become the ripples of our lives and our legacy. Each of us is given the opportunity to share our little fragment of time on this earth, and it is my greatest hope that I have used mine wisely.

We are the architects of our lives, and we all have the choice of accepting or rejecting life's challenges. Success is there for those who continue to pursue their dreams and persist. Orphaned or blind, my childlike faith allowed me to achieve success in spite of it all.

Many things that took place in my life just shouldn't have happened. My accomplishments were considerable and my blessings many, as I moved from a street-kid to a family man, a pauper to a prince, and a lone wolf to a shepherd for many. If I learned anything from my life experiences, it is that success in almost anything requires determination and tenacity — never giving up or giving in to the obstacles life may throw your way.

Life's meaning for me comes down to my wonderful family; friendships that in many instances have lasted a lifetime; the privilege of living in a free America; reaping the benefits and successes our country affords through education and business ventures; opportunities to pay back my debt to society; and the blessing of this era of modern science and technology that rescued me from the threat of blindness. Why wouldn't I consider myself a very blessed man? After all...

I was blind, but now I see.

Now, its your turn.

THE SHOCKING FACTS ABOUT
AGE-RELATED MACULAR DEGENERATION (AMD)

11–15 million **Estimated number of people with AMD today**
The number of people living with AMD today
is as great as the number of those
who have all types of invasive cancer

$9 **Dollars spent by NIH per AMD patient**

$461 **Dollars spent by NIH per Cancer patient**

50% **Estimated increase of AMD patients by 2020**

$350 billion **Estimated yearly global cost of visual
impairment due to Macular Degeneration**

$80 billion **Estimated yearly direct health care costs
related to Macular Degeneration in the US**

$1.3 billion **Amount paid by Medicare in 2013 for one
type of wet AMD injection (Ranibizumab)**

$100 million **Amount spent by NIH allotted for AMD in 2014**
Compare this to amounts spent on
Inflammatory Bowel Disease and Cancer (below)

$122 million **Amount spent by NIH allotted for
Inflammatory Bowel Disease in 2014**

$6 billion **Amount spent by NIH allotted
for Cancer in 2014**

PART I – AN OVERVIEW OF AMD

Introduction

Through the retelling of my story, I hope to have given you, the reader, an idea about how I reacted to and dealt with the diagnosis and eventual reality of macular degeneration. I did few things right along the way. But, my biggest mistake was not being more proactive in learning all I could about the disease, particularly in the early years. So, in this section I want to provide you with the information that I have learned along the way, information that, had I had it early on, might have helped me fare better through the years.

Expectations

As the human body ages, it naturally undergoes certain changes. A great many of these are accepted as par for the course. And while certain activities may have to be curtailed, or the level of participation in them adjusted, these realities do not seem to have the same impact as the prospect of macular degeneration and blindness.

As you know by now, football played a very big part in my life. As a football player, I always knew that the day would come when I would no longer have the physical capacity to play the game I so dearly loved. There is only so much stress a person's knees and back can take. While it was somewhat discouraging to be faced with these physical limitations, it was no surprise and I was well prepared for life after football. After recognizing and accepting that my football "career" was over, and realizing I still had a passion for the game, I began coaching. This way, I was able to stay deeply involved in the game, however from a changed perspective that took my physical limitations into account. Accepting these natural limits was not the end of my life; it was simply the end of one chapter and the beginning of the next — a chapter marked by new and unforgettable experiences. Dare I say that I enjoyed coaching more than playing?

Like my experience with football, most of us adjust constructively to the uncontrollable changes in life. As we get older, we realize we need a flashlight in order to see behind the television set, and the volume on that same TV seems to get softer, and so we turn it louder each year as we adjust to our ever-dulling hearing. We set the thermostat a degree or two higher as the years pass. We prefer driving during the day to driving at night and make our plans accordingly. We adjust our sleeping schedules, maybe working in a nap (or two!) during the day. All of this is normal and expected and does not do a great deal to offend our sense of individuality or reduce our satisfaction in life. And it is precisely because this deterioration of physical capacities is expected with aging, because we have been conditioned to accept these eventualities that we are able to cope with them relatively well. AMD, however, can be a shock and surprise. We are not prepared for it and thus it is hard for us to deal with it effectively.

Aging and the Human Eye

With age the human eye undergoes natural deteriorations. These include hardening and yellowing of the lens, which causes the sudden need in middle age for reading glasses and makes colors harder to identify. Other lens changes over time cause light to be scattered rather than focused precisely on the retina, which is why we have increasing difficulties with glare (i.e., all of those night driving issues). As we get older, we generally need more light to see than we did before, and objects become more difficult to identify. Quick movements and changes in the visual field can present challenges to vision. Our reaction time will also be slower, and this will normally be accompanied by a greater tendency to check and re-check the environment before making decisions that hinge on accurate visual perception of the surrounding environment (e.g., the cars around us on a highway or crowded public spaces). And the eyes of older people, particularly women after menopause, produce fewer tears, meaning a battle with "dry eye."

These changes, though frustrating at times and requiring adjustments both large and small, are normal and should be expected with aging. Most people expect to experience some degree of vision loss with age and accept the consequences of that. The normal changes wrought by aging do, indeed, require some lifestyle changes. But because we know about them, we are prepared for and accepting of them. If we have this same level of expectation and preparedness when facing AMD, we can meet its challenges with the same positive attitudes. Maintaining a high quality of life with AMD really boils down to having reasonable expectations about the disease and your life with it, while also being equipped with the information you need to make the most of your remaining vision.

What is AMD?

Age-related macular degeneration (AMD) is the leading cause of severe visual impairment and irreversible blindness in Americans over the age of fifty. The prevalence of AMD is nothing short of astonishing, especially considering how little the average person knows about it. At least eleven million Americans today have AMD, with nearly two million of those having the late-stage, advanced form of the disease. These numbers are expected to increase some fifty percent by 2020. America's rapidly aging population only heightens the urgency for disseminating information about AMD and working to create effective low vision rehabilitation programs to help millions of Americans achieve the highest quality of life possible.

What exactly is AMD? "Age-related macular degeneration is a late-onset, multifactorial neurodegenerative disease characterized by progressive degeneration of the photoreceptors/retinal pigment epithelial complex primarily in the macular region of the retina, resulting in irreversible central vision loss." Did you get that? No? Me either. Let's try it a different way.

Simply put, macular degeneration is a disease that impairs, and can even destroy, sharp central vision. Often slowly, and always painlessly, macular degeneration has the effect of clouding out crisp central images, making it difficult — perhaps eventually impossible — to read, to drive, to recognize faces, and to otherwise safely and independently navigate the surrounding environment. However, in the absence of any other visual dysfunction, peripheral vision remains intact.

To get a better handle on AMD, first we need to understand the eye and how vision works in general.

How Vision Works

A commonly used analogy to help illustrate how human vision works is to compare the eye with a camera (the old traditional film camera). Essentially it works like this: light enters the eye through the pupil (the camera's shutter); it is focused by the lens (the camera's lens), and is reflected onto the retina (the camera's film). Now, whereas the film of a camera holds the image, the retina produces chemical and electrical signals which are then carried through the optic nerve to the brain where the captured images are ultimately "developed" (perceived). The miracle of sight!

How AMD Affects Vision

So, what goes on with AMD to cause vision loss? Well, as the name implies, there is an ongoing process of degeneration of the macula of the eye. The macula is the part of the retina that is responsible for crisp central vision. Remember, light passing through the pupil and the lens is then focused back onto the retina. The retina, the film in our camera analogy, receives the whole image, but it is the macula that receives the parts of the images we view in our central line of sight. Now, even though a person has AMD, their eye still functions normally in that images are still focused back onto the retina as usual. However, the macula is compromised and so the image that is directed back onto it, the central image, is blurred, blackened, or in some way distorted. Think of a movie screen with a hole or a big black stain right in the middle of it. Even though the entire image is projected onto the screen, where the screen is compromised, the image will be also. So it goes with AMD.

The hallmark of AMD is the presence of drusen in the macula and retina more generally. These yellowish lesions have the effect of darkening the image directed back onto the retina, in turn producing a black spot (called a "scotoma"). AMD of this kind is commonly referred to as "dry." The "wet" form of AMD is characterized by problems with the blood vessels beneath the retina, which ultimately damage the macula. Perhaps a little more information will be helpful in aiding your understanding of the disease.

Dry AMD

Dry AMD is, by far, the most common form of the disease, accounting for roughly ninety percent of AMD cases. Dry AMD, though unpredictable in terms of severity and speed of progression, generally proceeds along a path of gradually decreasing central visual acuity. Somewhere between twelve and twenty-one percent of dry cases result in vision of 20/200 or worse. There are currently no treatments for dry AMD per se, but ongoing research may change that before too much longer. Lowering blood pressure and cholesterol levels if necessary, eating a diet high in micronutrients and antioxidants, and getting adequate exercise, may help slow the progression of the disease and decrease the likelihood of dry AMD becoming the more severe wet AMD. Certain nutritional supplements can help as well.

Wet AMD

While wet AMD accounts for just ten percent of all cases of AMD, ninety percent of the AMD patients who experience severe vision loss have wet AMD. Today, somewhere around two million Americans suffer from this form of the disease, characterized by the growth of abnormal blood vessels beneath the retina, which leads to bleeding and scarring in the macula, and thus visual impairment. If wet AMD is left untreated, it may progress rapidly.

There is no cure for wet AMD, either, but unlike dry AMD, there are many treatment options for it. These therapies can help preserve existing vision, reduce further vision loss, and even improve vision. Most common are injections of an anti-VEGF (vascular endothelial growth factor) agent, typically ranibizumab (Lucentis) or aflibercept (Eyelea) — both FDA approved, or bevacizumab (Avastin).

Lucentis and Avastin are drugs often used to treat colorectal cancer. Check with your specialist to learn more about the various treatment options and to determine which is right for you.

If I Have AMD, Does That Mean I Will Go Blind?

That AMD leads to central vision impairment does not mean that you are going to go totally blind. In fact, it is only the rare case of AMD that actually ends in profound blindness. Less than twenty percent of all AMD cases would be classified as late-stage, where AMD has reached something of a point of no return. However, even in many of those cases there are treatments, as described above, that can help you regain some degree of vision. For the majority of AMD cases, then, there are procedures that can help slow visual degradation as well as techniques that can help maximize existing vision for patients at all stages. So, in short, the answer to the above question is a resounding **"No!"**

What Is the Difference Between Blind, Legally Blind, and Low-Vision?

Blind, *legally blind*, and *low-vision* are quite different animals, and it is helpful to understand the nuances in these terms.

First, we should note that all people who are actually blind are legally blind, but not all legally blind people are totally blind. In fact, eighty-five percent of legally blind Americans maintain some degree of functional vision. Legally blind is actually a governmental term that signifies that someone's BCVA (best corrected visual acuity) is less than 20/200 or is restricted to a visual field of less than twenty degrees. Because of their visual limitations, these people are then able to receive certain governmental assistance, including tax benefits and access to local assistive programs.

However, these same people often live very active and fulfilling lives despite their compromised visual acuity.

Low vision more accurately describes most AMD patients. Medicare recognizes a person with BCVA of 20/60 in their better-seeing eye as eligible to receive coverage for low vision services. Low vision, then, is not the same thing as no vision. It is simply not the case that most AMD sufferers are totally or functionally blind; rather they live with vision that is less than optimal, less than 20/20. In positive terms, this means that AMD patients can often still function quite well and participate in many activities and hobbies. Indeed, the majority of those who currently have some form of AMD would not even be classified as having low vision. Furthermore, recent developments in treatments of AMD have been shown to reduce cases terminating in legal blindness by fifty percent. Ultimately, the message here is hope. Even with AMD, a high quality of life can be maintained.

Am I at Risk for AMD?

AMD is largely unpredictable; however, certain factors make it more likely that you will develop it. These can be divided into two broad categories: uncontrollable and controllable.

Uncontrollable Risk Factors
- Age
- Race (Caucasians are more susceptible)
- Family history (genetic predisposition)
- Light eye color
- Low macular pigment

Because these factors are entirely uncontrollable, it is probably sufficient to just highlight a few key stats. At fifty-five years of age, the odds of you showing some early signs of AMD are about fourteen percent. By age seventy-five, the chances increase to thirty percent that you are experiencing or will experience some form of AMD, and seven percent that you have full-blown macular degeneration (either wet or dry). The majority of AMD sufferers in America are Caucasian (eighty-nine percent of cases, compared to four percent Hispanic, three percent African-American, and four percent other). Indeed, genetics have proven to be a key indicator in the development of AMD, and studies are progressing down this trail in the hunt for a cure.

Controllable Risk Factors
- Smoking (former or current)
- Cardiovascular health
- Obesity
- Sunlight exposure

If you are presently a smoker, stop! The single most important preventative measure you can take to decrease your risk of developing AMD is to stop smoking. In fact, smoking alone leads to a threefold increased risk of the disease. It is never too late to stop smoking, so do it today. Studies confirm that twenty years after quitting, former smokers no longer face an increased risk of developing AMD.

Here, too, proper diet (including lots of green, leafy vegetables) and exercise are also linked to decreases in the development of AMD. This is one more reason that regular exercise of some sort needs to be part of your regime.

AREDS supplements (see below) may also reduce the risk of getting the disease. Finally, it is always beneficial to wear a broad-brimmed hat and sunglasses in outdoor environments, particularly if you have light-colored eyes. If these glasses are to be of any value, however, the lenses must block both UV and blue light rays, and wraparound styles are best.

Is AMD Preventable?

Early detection is not a preventative measure per se. However, since it is possible to stem the tide, so to speak, of macular degeneration, it is vitally important that you: monitor your eyesight regularly, have regular eye examinations, and inform your doctor as soon as you notice any changes in visual performance. Your doctor can tell you how often your regular appointments and checkups should take place.

EARLY DETECTION AND INTERVENTION

Early detection is not a preventative measure per se.
However, since it is possible to stem
the tide, so to speak, of macular degeneration,
it is vitally important that you:
monitor your eyesight regularly; have regular
eye examinations; and inform your
doctor as soon as you notice any changes
in visual performance.
Your doctor can tell you how often
your regular appointments
and checkups should take place.

WJ Hindman

The Amsler Grid

A key assessment tool in early detection of AMD is the Amsler Grid. Only your doctor can tell you exactly how *you* should be using this tool, but here are the basics of general use.

- Secure the grid somewhere on a level viewing field about fourteen inches from your face.
- If you normally wear glasses for reading, keep them on. If not, do not wear them.
- Cover either your left or right eye.
- With the uncovered eye, focus on the dot at the center of the grid.
- Repeat with the other eye.

If you look at this grid...

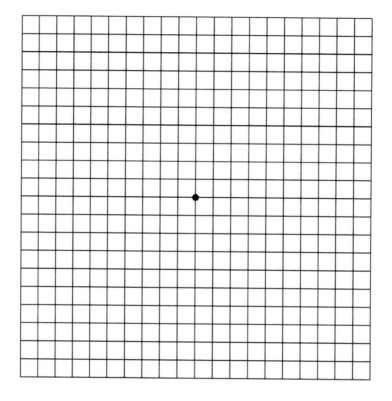

**...and you see wavy, blurry, or missing lines,
it's a signature of AMD.**

*If you notice any distorted, blurred, missing, or wavy lines
you should contact your eye care specialist (ophthalmologist)
immediately!*

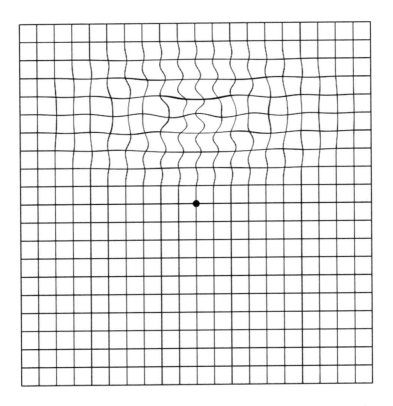

AREDS Vitamin

AREDS: this is a term you are going to come across a lot in the world of AMD. AREDS stands for Age Related Eye Disease Study. This study, sponsored by the National Eye Institute, was designed to learn more about the natural history and risk factors of age-related macular degeneration and cataract and to evaluate the effect of high doses of vitamin C, vitamin E, beta-carotene, and zinc on the progression of AMD and cataracts. There has subsequently been a second study, AREDS 2, which was designed to test several formulation variants based on the original AREDS findings.

The big outcome of these studies is that the AREDS formulation (see below) significantly lowers the chance of the progression of early and intermediate AMD to neovascular ("wet") AMD. Some evidence exists that shows that diets high in these AREDS formulation antioxidants can even reduce the risk of developing early AMD in persons otherwise genetically predisposed to it. However, the AREDS studies themselves only show that the formulation is effective in slowing the progress of AMD development.

AREDS:
- Vitamin C – 500 mg
- Vitamin E – 400 IU
- Beta-carotene – 15 mg
- Zinc – 80 mg
- Copper – 2 mg

AREDS 2 introduced lutein and zeaxanthin and eliminated beta-carotene. Studies continually point to the benefit of lutein for increased visual performance, and many researchers (though not all) believe a formulation containing meso-zeaxanthin, lutein, and zeaxanthin (in a 10:10:2 ratio) will greatly improve visual performance. Bausch and Lomb is one of several premier manufacturers of various vision nutritional supplements, including AREDS and AREDS 2 formulations. The Baush and Lomb online community, the Joy of Sight Club (joyofsight.com), provides free educational resources about AMD and coupons for their supplements. Do be sure that you check with your doctor before beginning any supplementation program, as high levels of certain vitamins and antioxidants have been known to increase the risk of other potentially fatal diseases, including cancer, elsewhere in the body.

AREDS 2:
- Vitamin C – 500 mg
- Vitamin E – 400 IU
- Zinc – 80 mg
- Copper – 2 mg
- Lutein – 10 mg
- Zeaxanthin – 2 mg

PART II – AN OVERVIEW OF THE IMT

What is the IMT?

The IMT™, designed by Dr. Isaac Lipshitz and his partner Yossi Gross, is manufactured by VisionCare Ophthalmic Technologies, and distributed through their CentraSight program. The device, a miniature Galilean telescope which is surgically implanted into the eye, received FDA approval in July 2010 for patients seventy-five years and older. And, thanks to the persistence of VisionCare CEO Allen Hill coupled with my own efforts, which included raising public awareness and lobbying a number of politicians, in October 2014 the FDA approved the device for patients as young as sixty-five, a huge win for AMD sufferers across America. The device is covered by Medicare and many private insurance companies for those patients who meet the rather specific criteria for implantation.

What Does the IMT Do?

As a telescope, the IMT™ works with the optics of the cornea to direct back onto the retina images in the central sight, at a scale of 2.2x or 2.7x their actual size. By magnifying the images, the scotoma (the black spot which disturbs vision) becomes relatively less meaningful. The scotoma does not actually change size; it is merely smaller in comparison to the rest of the IMT™-enlarged image (see below).

The patient, through practice and exercise, learns to focus on central images with the IMT™ eye while using the fellow eye (the non-implanted eye) for context, using existing peripheral vision. One downside of the IMT™ surgery is that the patient loses peripheral vision in the implanted eye. So patients need to, in a sense, learn to see again, using each eye for different functions.

Who Is the IMT For?

People who are sixty-five years old or older:
- who have end-stage AMD with central blind spots in both eyes, and no active formation of new blood vessels associated with AMD
- whose vision is not correctable by other means
- who have not had cataract surgery in both eyes
- who have adequate peripheral vision in the eye that would not receive the implant
- whose vision improves significantly while using an external telescope simulator
- whose vision goals are realistic and achievable
- who feel they can become accustomed to a difference in vision between their eyes
- who have a good chance of useful improvement in their everyday activities and living
- are willing and able to work with low vision specialists for visual training/rehabilitation after the surgery

There are other more technical — perhaps "medical" is a better word — considerations that ultimately determine a person's viability as a candidate for the IMT™, and an eye-care specialist can provide information on these.

To summarize, if you have already had cataract surgery in both eyes, the IMT™ is not an option for you. If you are not ready to commit to practicing with the IMT™ every day for anywhere between a few months to two years, if you think the IMT™ is going to restore your vision one hundred percent, or if you are able to find alternative, nonsurgical solutions that enable you to participate in the activities you enjoy the most, then the IMT™ might not be right for you.

If, however, you realize that the IMT™ is just one treatment option that has, with dedicated commitment to a rehabilitation program, the potential to restore your vision to a point where you can begin enjoying many activities again, then the IMT™ might just be right for you.

What Can the IMT Do for Me?

While the IMT™ is effective in most cases, people with the implant will experience varying degrees of progress and success, and therefore varying satisfaction. From the start, it must be remembered that the IMT™ does not promise to restore your vision exactly as it was before you had AMD. It is a treatment, not a cure. The clinical trials showed that the majority of patients (approximately sixty percent) experienced an increase of BCVA (best corrected visual acuity — the best you can see with corrective glasses) greater than or equal to three lines of vision on the wall chart at the two-year mark. Seventy-five percent of patients gained at least two lines.

If you are expecting *more* than that level of improvement, and you spend several months, even up to two years, practicing and exercising your new vision, it is likely that you will be dissatisfied with the results and may end up more depressed than if you had not gotten the surgery in the first place. I have said it already, but it bears repeating: successfully living with AMD requires *reasonable expectations* coupled with the *motivation* to do what is within your control to achieve the highest standard of living possible. Unreasonable expectations will nearly always lead to dissatisfaction. And dissatisfaction will only work to make your low vision rehabilitation that much less successful, and your quality of life will be lower because of it.

Through a feature story on *NBC News* with Brian Williams I was fortunate enough to meet several other IMT™ patients, and it has been mutually beneficial for us to share our experiences and encourage one another. Tom Sarver, for example, was one of the first IMT™ patients ever, involved in the clinical trial of this device. Tom had immediate success with the implant and excelled so quickly that his rehabilitation team did not know what to make of his progress. His "natural" adaptation to the device rendered much of the post-operation activity superfluous.

On the other hand, Anne Montefusco, an IMT™ patient whose story also appeared on television, has not experienced the early successes of Tom Sarver, or even the slower but steady progress I myself have experienced. Thankfully, she was able to connect with my team and me, and with the support and reassurance of her occupational therapist, she has been encouraged to press on.

Between the experiences of Tom, immediately successful, and Anne, struggling after months, there is my own, fairly comfortable after two years. And so, even with just those stories, if you are considering the IMT™, you now have a much better idea of what you can expect going into it. This is obviously not the final word on the IMT™, and I do not purport that our experiences are entirely typical. Results vary. Again, it all comes down to *expectation*, what you hope to get out of it, and *motivation*, how much work you are willing to put into it.

Where Can I Go to Get the IMT?

New IMT™ implant centers are opening all the time, and you can call or email CentraSight to find the one nearest you: 1-877-997-4448, http://www.centrasight.com/appointment.

PART III – LIVING WELL WITH LOW VISION

The first thing you need when diagnosed with AMD, and preferably before, is information. Still, even more important than the what of AMD is the how. How do I live the highest quality of life in spite of my visual impairment? The answers to both the what and how of AMD fall under the umbrella of Low Vision Rehabilitation (LVR). The goal of LVR is to educate and empower those experiencing low vision in order that they might have the highest possible quality of life.

Time to Make a Choice

Loss of some degree of vision is a present reality for some, an inevitable future for many, and an impending, though perhaps treatable, challenge for millions more. Here the expression "reality follows perception" is true. If you are in any one of those categories, you have a choice: you can allow your perception of what is going to be a "diminished" and "degraded" life to negatively control your reality; or, you can envision all the possibilities and opportunities that still exist and maintain a positive perception of the reality that, while your vision may be impaired, you are still filled with life!

To keep a positive attitude through your struggles with AMD, you need to know what to expect. This is particularly true because depression caused by vision loss is often tied directly to expectations. And in a vicious cycle, depression actually decreases the effectiveness of low vision rehabilitation, making further depression even more likely. Studies have shown that success in low vision rehabilitation is related to psychosocial factors, including "depression, satisfaction with life, social support, self-esteem, stress, and motivation."

In order to meet your needs, then, it is recommended that a low vision rehabilitation program include (at minimum) elements of: education about the disease, expectations about living with low vision, information to improve visual performance and increase independence, and identification of helpful resources.

Learning about Rehabilitation Services

It is possible to self-administer an LVR program, but it is far better to have assistance. Presently, there is an overwhelming lack of assistive programs for low vision sufferers. However, the landscape is not completely barren. The Lions Clubs International, for example, is committed to providing low vision services to citizens around the world.

The Lions Clubs' Website Provides the Following List of Services for the Visually Impaired:

- Supporting guide dog schools
- Scholarships for blind students
- Supporting vocational training programs
- Facilitating self-help groups for the blind/visually impaired
- Furnishing talking books, Braille books, and large-print books for public libraries
- Supporting recreational activities and Lions camps for individuals who are blind or have severe vision loss
- Providing devices such as white canes, braillers (Braille "typewriters"), or computers
- Funding eye research

Further, my local Lions Club (Multiple District 22: Maryland, Delaware, and D.C.) is creating, in partnership with the Lions Vision Research and Rehabilitation Center at Johns Hopkins Wilmer Eye Institute, and the help of a grant from Reader's Digest Partners for Sight Foundation, a community-based healthcare program designed to connect low vision sufferers with low vision service providers. Certainly this is an essential step in meeting the needs of an ever-growing low vision and AMD population.

Tips for More Independent Living

You should definitely consult with a professional who can recommend a LVR program that is tailored to your specific needs. Short of that, however, what follows is an overview of some general ideas about low vision rehabilitation that should help start you on your journey towards a brighter future.

Maximizing Existing Vision

Vision training, though useful in general, is best when it is targeted to individual needs. One of the keys to determining what exercises or techniques you should learn and practice is deciding which activities are most important to you and you would like most to keep doing. For example, an IMT™ patient in England wanted the surgery specifically so she could keep bowling. Therefore, her needs were specific and her training and rehab could be customized to meet her desired end. Is it reading you are most interested in? Playing bridge? Watching television? It's entirely up to you decide and that will enable you make a plan that will help you reach your goals.

FINDING THE "SWEET SPOT"

When you have AMD, generally, a large black blind spot
called a scotoma appears somewhere
in your field of view. Fortunately, it is possible to retrain
your eyes, to some degree, to ignore it,
or at least not focus on it.

There are a number of techniques or exercises for this.
Some are fun and some are work,
but all are helpful. If you are fortunate enough to have
the help of an occupational therapist
or other low vision specialist, hopefully they will show you
some of these. However, if you are more
or less on your own, the exercise on the following pages
will get you started.

**The goal is to be able to view clearly, and at will, the circle at the center of the clock below.
Start by looking at (fixing your vision on) the circle at the center.**

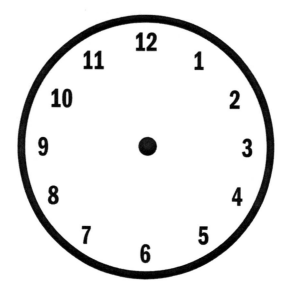

- It is likely that the center of the circle will be obscured by the scotoma. If not, the numbers that are blurred will indicate where your scotoma is located. Do this several times until you have firmly established exactly where your scotoma is.

- Now, start by looking at the number one (even if you cannot see it, the idea is to move your vision towards that region of the clock), and see if you are able to see the center circle more clearly. If not, move onto looking at two, then three, and so on, until you have found the places in your field of vision where, if you shift your focus there, you can see the center of the circle more clearly.

- Once you have identified this spot on the clock, practice focusing your vision there, so that when an object enters your central vision, you can quickly make the visual adjustments necessary to see it more clearly.

In this exercise you are learning to "move" your scotoma out of the way so you can achieve some level of central vision. If you practice viewing the world in this way, you can still successfully perceive the objects that appear in the center of your visual field.

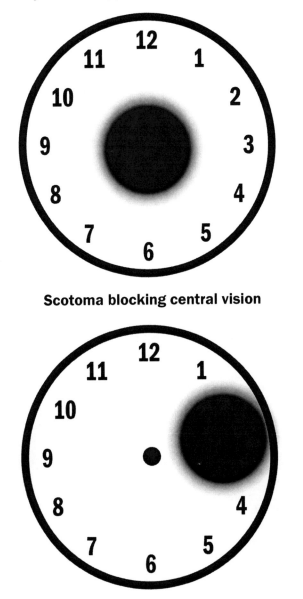

Scotoma blocking central vision

Scotoma moved out of central vision by looking between 2 and 3

Using Peripheral Vision

The IMT™ is designed to restore some level of central vision in the eye in which it is implanted. However, this is only at the cost of whatever existing peripheral vision you may have in that eye. And so, the other, fellow eye will be used for peripheral vision. In this way, each eye is functioning independently, but together. Even if you do not go the route of getting the IMT™, you will still find it useful to learn how to use your peripheral vision. In either case, as you encounter environments, especially those new and unfamiliar, you will receive most of your initial information through your peripheral vision. Take advantage of this by slowing down long enough so that you are able to establish some context for your surroundings. Even though it is not as finely detailed as central vision, the information you receive from your peripheral vision is important for successful navigation.

Putting It Together: Scanning

Scanning is useful not just for IMT™ patients but all AMD sufferers. Scanning puts together the practices of "moving" your scotoma and taking advantage of your peripheral vision. As you enter an environment or interact with something of interest (for example a newspaper), you should start by moving your eyes all around in order to take in the "big picture." This rapid movement of your eyes is called *scanning*. Scanning is critical, especially in unfamiliar environments.

• First, you are going to want to take a few seconds to really move your eyes around, seeing the whole picture by scanning as much of the environment as possible. Avoid excessive movement of the head as you scan, since you may just end up bringing your scotoma along with you everywhere you look!

- Next, as you scan, if you have identified an object of particular interest, a person or paragraph for example, you will want to move your focus to that. As you do, of course, you will most likely find that the object is obscured by your scotoma.
- Now you can employ the clock method in order to bring the desired object into better focus.

Certainly these techniques do require practice. This is a whole new way of viewing the world around you, and it will likely take time to become proficient at it. There are several steps required for mastery. What is more, if you have a central scotoma, or are getting used to your IMT™, you are going to find it even more difficult, as you will have to really work on integrating that clock method into your visual practices. Nevertheless, do not give up. Every day people are taking advantage of skills like this and are living active lives as a result. You can too!

Reading

Not being able to read effectively can be particularly troubling. Reading demands and expectations vary from person to person. Likewise, the ability to read various things, along with the techniques and equipment necessary to do so, are just as diverse. There are many types of reading, including recreational (reading a book), professional (reading documents and internet data), and casual (reading labels and menus). Only after determining the actual scope and nature of an activity are you able to make a wise decision as to what assistive device, if any, you need to continue participation in it.

To personalize the process of reading improvement, there are several questions you should ask yourself: What is my current reading ability? What are my reading needs (leisure, work, necessity)? What are my reading goals (comprehension, enjoyment)? Where do I read most of the time? What equipment do I already have that could help me read better? By just answering these few questions you should be on your way toward creating and meeting your reading goals.

If you must read for work, for example, your goal will be to become as proficient at reading as you can, given your limitations. You will probably need to make the most of good lighting, magnification equipment, and proper positioning. If, on the other hand, you are merely a casual reader you would do well to consider alternatives, such as audio books.

Equipment

Over the course of these past twenty or so years, as I searched for the right equipment to help me live with low vision I spent . . . well, I spent a lot (over $13,000 just for the items listed below)! I wanted to be able to watch television, read books, use the computer, make phone calls, and navigate independently. Through the years I purchased sunglasses, safety glasses, distance glasses, binoculars, monoculars, CCTVs, handheld magnifiers, big screen computer monitors, eye charts, talking watches, talking clocks, talking scales, low vision pens, low vision notepads — you name it, I bought it! If there was an assist I heard about or could find anywhere, especially anything that would make print larger and easier to read, it was soon on its way to me.

Here is a list of some of those purchases, along with prices:

- CCTV – Optelec: $3,195.00
- Video Eye: $2,250.00
- Ruby – portable video eye: $545.00
- Optelec Reader: $1,795.00
- Distance glasses: $1,475.00
- Intermediate glasses: $1,475.00
- Bifocals: $657.40
- Safety glasses: $110.00
- Sports glasses with varying magnification that reduces field width as magnification increases: $130.89
- Reading glasses with rechargeable LED lights built into frames: $396.00
- Sunglasses that go over regular glasses: $544.93
- Handheld spot 5x magnifier on neck lanyard: $7.50
- Handheld spot 8x magnifier with light: $24.95
- Eye patch with stretchable band: $5.97
- AREDS vitamins, per month: $15.00
- PreserVision vitamins, per month: $15.00
- Eye charts, Amsler (Free internet download)
- Eye charts, letters and numbers (Free internet download)
- Orange paint to mark objects: $10.00
- Orange tape for stairs: $10.00
- Kitchen timer to keep track of practice sessions: $10.00
- Ott® lamps with very bright bulbs: $200.00
- Talking watch: $43.95
- Talking clock: $24.95
- Talking scale: $49.99
- Folding long cane: $22.40
- Telescoping long cane with belt holder: $56.39
- Low vision notebooks (notebooks with extra-bold lines with more space between them): $5.95
- 20/20 pens (A felt-tip pen that is extra wide and has bold black ink. I like it and it helps me to read my own writing): $1.19

I learned quickly (perhaps not quickly enough!) that not all equipment is created equal and not all equipment is equally helpful or necessary. Furthermore, finding the right equipment also includes locating things that have little to do with visual performance as such. Entire catalogs of items designed specifically for people living with low vision exist, items like mitts for ironing to avoid being burned, plates with lips to minimize spilling, and mobility aids from canes to scooters.

I was fortunate enough to be able to purchase all this equipment through the years, but I want to help save you the expense and frustration of repeating my mistakes. That is why you must determine what your needs are and then figure out how best to meet those needs. Despite your specific needs, however, it is likely that in one way or another, at one time or another, if you have AMD and are dealing with low vision, you are probably going to find the need for magnification, both optical and non-optical.

Optical Magnification

Optical magnification is as it sounds: equipment intended to increase the size of something visually. Broadly, optical magnification can be further subdivided into categories of portability. For example, a standard portable magnifier would be a handheld magnifying glass on a lanyard, something you can take with you everywhere, used to read labels on products in the supermarket or a menu at a restaurant. A stationary device would be something like the Optelec Reader™ which turns text into speech. Again, personal needs should determine what equipment you purchase.

Non-optical Magnification

Non-optical magnification has to do with things which, though normally small, have been purposefully enlarged or changed in some other way to aid in low vision: large-print books, phones and remote controls with enlarged numbers, large calendars, and so forth. These items are usually relatively inexpensive, easy-to-use, and are great alternatives for people with low vision.

Additional Accessories

Items such as talking watches, clocks, and scales, large felt-tip pens for writing, and low vision notebooks are also quite useful. All these assistive devices help add normalcy to a life of low vision.

Computers

Computers can be a great asset for people with low vision. Computers allow users to change brightness, contrast, typeface, and size to customize the viewing experience for each user and overcome some of the limitations of low vision. E-books can be read directly on a computer screen, and if you have a twenty-inch monitor or larger, you should be able to read these relatively easily despite your otherwise compromised vision. Many websites, especially those aimed toward the senior population, allow users to change contrast and font size on any page also. The operating system of your computer (for example, Windows if you have a PC) will also likely have a feature that can translate the contents of the page you are viewing into speech (in Windows this is called "Narrator").

There are also software programs which can help you navigate a website if you are experiencing profound vision loss. For example, the software will read aloud the contents of the page and actively guide you as you explore the page with your mouse. "The link for AMD information is a little to the left. A little more. Yes, click now." Additionally, there is periphery equipment which can make the computer even more valuable to low vision sufferers, such as devices which will project documents onto the computer screen, making them easier to view.

Other Emerging Technologies

Every year evolving technology is producing more and better aids for the visually handicapped, of which the following are only a few examples.

UpSense Keyboard

The Israeli company Inpris developed UpSense, a mobile app with the first fully gesture-based keyboard to enable people with visual impairment to type on tablets and smartphones using customizable gestures. The app also has a mode for those already proficient in Braille typing.

Project RAY

Project RAY, the world's first smartphone for people with visual disabilities, debuted in Israel and was launched in the U.S. in 2014 in collaboration with Qualcomm, Amazon, and T-Mobile. The device uses advanced smartphone technologies (multiple sensors, camera, compass, and audio) and communication services (phone, messaging, and cloud) to give users greater independence and accessibility to essential digital services.

The ForeseeHome AMD Monitor

The Tel Aviv-based company Notal Vision, founded by a team of Israeli eye doctors in 2000, has produced the first teleconnected home-based system to monitor age-related macular degeneration between eye exams, allowing for earlier detection of important visual changes. The system posts the patient's current data on a secure website where a physician can review it at any time. In 2009, Notal got FDA approval for this device, called the ForeseeHome AMD Monitor, which is a great advancement and will help tremendously in the early diagnosis of macular degeneration. This monitor is sold out of the company's new U.S. headquarters in Chantilly, Virginia.

Living with Low Vision: Environmental Modification

Apart from maximizing your existing vision or, better yet, in tandem with it, modifying your environment will prove to be the best investment of time and energy in your fight to live well with AMD. Improving lighting, getting your home and each room in it organized along with all the things in those rooms, and adding safety features in general will be most beneficial to your feeling of independence. These changes do not have to be dramatic or expensive to be helpful. In fact, the most useful modifications will cost little more than a little time and effort. The suggestions that follow are meant only as examples — ideas to get the creative juices flowing.

Lighting and Contrast

Few changes will be as helpful as incorporating the proper lighting into your home, making full use of both artificial and natural light. Natural light is, of course, sunlight; artificial light includes all the different light types: incandescent, halogen, and fluorescent. Each of these has its own advantages and disadvantages.

Sunlight is perhaps the best light and allows most people to see the most. However, there is the possibility of glare, which can negatively affect vision. Incandescent bulbs are affordable, but they are getting harder to find, and they do not, particularly at the lower wattage (less than 100), provide adequate lighting in many situations. At higher wattages the light is normally sufficient, but the bulbs get very hot. Halogen bulbs are great for intimate workspaces, such as desks or hobby tables, because they are so bright. But they get even hotter, which is a consideration. Fluorescents are also quite bright, but they usually call for a different type of fixture, and some people do not like the color or noise of many fluorescents.

The key concept to remember when it comes to lighting is *contrast*. The greater the contrast between the object you want to see and its surroundings, the better you will be able to see the desired object. Of course, generally speaking, the brighter the area the better all around. However, when it comes to doing specific chores or tasks, the greater the contrast between what you are working on and the environment around it, the better. Creating contrast can be done with proper lighting and also the colors of things.

When it comes to reading or hobbying, it is particularly helpful to establish an area or areas specifically designed for that task. Natural lighting is helpful and general room lighting also. However, by adding task-specific lighting you will effectively increase contrast and find reading or hobbying much easier and more enjoyable.

Posture and position count for a lot also. You want to create an environment where you can sit comfortably with good posture and that places the material you are working on or reading at the most convenient and effective distance. It is absolutely essential that you equip that area with task-specific lighting. On a table or desk, this could be a desk lamp with any of the aforementioned bulb types. In an armchair or the like, it might be a floor lamp with the light directed immediately onto the viewing material.

When you are not engaging in specific chores or tasks, and for daily living in general, it is best to have light spread evenly throughout each room. This will require a combination of natural light, using blinds or shades, and artificial light, strategically placed in each room. Each room requires its own particular lighting, depending on the activities that will take place there. In the bedroom, lighting aimed at a mirror and in closets is helpful. In the kitchen, lighting over the oven and especially the food preparation area will help you avoid injury. In the dining room, good lighting over the table will add to your enjoyment of meals. Good lighting over all stairways is key to avoiding missteps.

Don't forget outside lights. Install them everywhere you need them, and use them. After dark, make sure that all of the outside lights are on if you plan to travel outside.

A final note on contrast. Contrast does not just have to do with lighting; this concept can be incorporated into nearly every facet of daily living. Eating light-colored foods on dark plates, marking electric outlets with bright tape, hanging a dark shower curtain and dark towels in a white bathroom (for that matter using brightly colored soap in your light-colored tub) — you get the idea.

The principle of contrast can also be carried over to how you organize your home, each room, and the items within it. The more "stuff" you have lying around your home or in drawers, the less contrast there is, and so the more difficult it is to see and to navigate safely.

Creative Strategies for Coping

In adjusting to low vision, you will likely have to find new ways of doing everyday tasks. You will have to use creativity and experiment until you find what works for you. Maybe the new way will involve fancy gizmos, or maybe it will require just a few simple tricks and common household items put to new inventive uses.

Bright Tape and Puff Paint

Bright-colored tape will also help add contrast to your environment and ease your travels. Marking steps with fluorescent-colored tape is quite useful. Bright tape can also help you to locate electric outlets, remote controls, and other otherwise hard-to-see objects.

Likewise, brightly colored puff paint works to cheaply and effectively modify everyday items for easy use. You can purchase this type of paint in hobby shops — it comes in a variety of eye-catching colors — and when it dries, it is puffy, adding texture. Because it adds not only color but textural contrast, you will likely find it indispensable. Marking the "minute" button on the microwave, the "on" button on the stereo with one color, and the "play" button with another, and marking the cap of medications with the spot where it must be aligned are all practical uses for puff paint which make living with low vision that much easier.

Other Practical Tips

Counting steps is also a great coping strategy. Knowing how many stairs there are, how many steps from the bedroom to the bathroom, from the front door to the mailbox, is a simple trick that can help you feel more in control when navigating independently.

When buying new furniture, choose textured fabrics to help you identify things, but avoid patterns like checks or stripes that can be visually confusing. Make sure area rugs are securely taped down and that electrical cords are out of the way. Use nightlights in bedrooms, bathrooms, and hallways. Don't wax the floors. Keep smoke detectors powered and operational. You should also institute a policy immediately: all doors are, at all times, to be kept either all the way opened or all the way closed; there is no in between.

Decluttering

Decluttering your home is one of the biggest and most cost effective improvements you can make. It is critical that all the main thoroughfares in your home, especially, are clutter-free, and kept that way. The risk of falls is greatly increased with low vision, and decluttering your home will help reduce that risk. Again, decluttering closets and dressers will help in getting dressed and putting clothes and other items away. To this last point, everything in your home should have its assigned place and each time an item is used, that item should be returned to that spot. This practice will help keep your home clean and will decrease the frustration of looking for something that has been misplaced.

Organizing the Bedroom

It's time to finally make those tough choices. You may need to get rid of a bunch of clothes that no longer fit or you no longer use, but the least you should do is organize what you have. Get into that sock-drawer and throw away all those "mismatchers." Better yet, buy a bunch of socks that are the same kind and same color. That will make dressing and laundry much easier. Underwear and other items should be neatly stacked in their drawers and always returned to the same place. Can't tell your navy blue slacks from the black ones? Put a small safety pin on the waistband of the navy. Put matching outfits together on one hanger. Find a place for shoes to be put away, perhaps in a hanging shoe organizer. Nothing goes on the floor except the furniture. And keep a flashlight on your nightstand.

Organizing the Kitchen

Your kitchen may indeed be ground zero for your organization efforts. It will help to minimize your collection of knives, bowls, and measuring cups, not to mention organizing, once and for all, the stuff in that "junk" drawer.

In the kitchen you may also find bright puff paint particularly helpful. As noted earlier, you can use it to mark the "minute" button on the microwave and the "start" button on the dishwasher.

Additionally, keep cabinet and cupboard drawers and doors shut after you retrieve an item — especially the dishwasher door. Keep handles of pots and pans turned toward the center of the stove, to avoid burns. You can also mark pot and pan handles with brightly colored tape. And tie back long hair or loose clothing when cooking. Keep food items in the same location every time you shop. If it's hard to tell two items apart, such as chicken noodle soup and chicken rice soup, put a rubber band around one of them (then, try to remember which one it is!).

Organizing the Bathroom

This is the room where you will have to perhaps invest the most money, though hopefully still not much. Depending on your level of vision loss, you may find it very beneficial to install safety bars around the toilet and in the shower stall. These small investments will pay for themselves over and over again if they save you from even a single fall. Take seriously the risks of living with low vision, particularly in an area that naturally predisposes people to slipping and falling. A rubber mat that contrasts with the tub bottom is worth considering, as is one of the specially designed plastic tub or shower chairs.

Another eyesight-aiding tip for the bathroom is asking your pharmacy to put large-print labels on any medications you may be taking.

What Next?

It would take a lot of space to describe all the tips and techniques that exist to prepare your home for low vision. Hopefully, apart from the practical suggestions offered, your mind has been actively formulating ways in which you might modify your own environment to help you better navigate in it.

Letting Others Help

Organizations like the Lions Clubs International and their local clubs exist to help people just like you. There are people standing by right now who can help. Let them!

Tips If You Are the Helper

Here are some suggestions for maximizing helpfulness and avoiding hassles.

Do's

- If you are the caregiver of someone with AMD or low vision for any reason, have patience. Vision loss is a difficult adjustment for both the person affected and his/her loved ones and caregivers. Try to put yourself in the patient's shoes.
- Help the person choose matching clothes. Depending on the degree of vision loss, it may even be helpful to have them purchase, for example, socks of just two colors: black and white. This makes dressing much easier. A similar strategy can be used for other undergarments as well as shirts and pants.
- Store different types of clothes in the same place all the time. This is true for pretty much everything in the house. Everything should have its own designated spot. If you use or move something, make sure it gets put back in the same place you took it from.
- Offer to help rearrange the person's home to make it safer and more accessible.
- When walking with someone with low vision, point out differences in the path, especially changes in elevation such as steps and curbs.
- If the person takes medications, set them up in a weekly pill box. You might also consider marking each day with a different color sticker or puff paint.
- At doctors' offices, the staff will often give a patient with low vision things to sign. They just hand the person the paper and say, "Sign this, please." Then the patient has to search the page. Make sure that whoever hands the person a paper like this points to exactly where he/she should sign. And clearly explain the document that is being signed.
- Encourage and help low vision sufferers to stay active. Perhaps the worst thing people with low vision can do is nothing.

- Help low vision sufferers take advantage of low vision rehabilitation and low vision services in their local area. Low vision rehabilitation can help patients maintain and maximize their existing vision, helping them function in new ways. And in many cases services are free. These services might include basic low vision training or car services that will take low vision sufferers to medical appointments or the supermarket.

Don'ts
- Don't overdo helpfulness and solicitousness. If there is something the person can do for him or herself, let them do it. Don't make them feel like an invalid.
- Don't feel sorry for them and let it show, so that you end up doing too much for them. Don't let your compassion come across the wrong way — either as a signal that they are doomed and should just give up now, or as a permission slip for them to let you wait on them hand and foot.
- At the same time, don't assume that the person is entirely functional or self-sufficient. Many people are too proud to admit that they can't do the things they used to. So don't be afraid to step in and help out.
- Don't lose your cool. Your charge is frustrated with his or her limitations, and dealing with stages of grief that may surface at any time. Add to this the problem of possible miscommunications, and it's easy to see why tempers can sometimes flare. So try to be calm and understanding at all times.
- Don't forget to have empathy. Understand that experiencing low vision can be devastating both physically and mentally. What low vision sufferers often need most is someone with a warm heart, a listening ear, and a willing spirit.

PART IV – IT ISN'T WHERE YOU START, IT'S WHERE YOU FINISH!

Through my battle with AMD I went through the many phases of grief: denial (not me), depression (what difference does anything make?), and withdrawal (why bother?). In the beginning, I was caught up in a combination of all three of these negative feelings and actions, but I was eventually saved by my lifelong philosophy of never, never giving up.

Don't let self-imposed, self-limiting thoughts get to you. Any time we say, "I can't" to ourselves, and fail to try for fear of not making it, we are limiting ourselves.

When I was diagnosed with AMD, I thought I was going to go completely blind and there was nothing I could do about it. And that is the future I almost surrendered to. Back then, I did not have any information or education about maximizing my existing vision, so as my vision loss progressed I just let it, assuming blindness was a foregone conclusion. How I wish I had known even the few techniques offered above. I can only imagine the difference that would have made on my life for those long, dark years.

Living with AMD requires you to relearn how to view the world. It can be challenging, but it is at least as rewarding to know that with the right equipment and enough motivation, you can continue to live actively and enjoy the activities that bring you pleasure.

I wish I had known even ten percent of what I know now when I was first diagnosed with AMD. I am sure I would have lived a more satisfying life those many years where I essentially surrendered to my diagnosis. I hope you have been encouraged to take action, to learn all you can, and to make the necessary modifications in your life and your home to help you maintain a high quality of life.

Appendices

Here you will find: definitions of key terms related to AMD, contact information for a variety of helpful resources, a list of recommended reading, and the bibliography. I hope these may prove a valuable guide and reference for you.

Appendix 1 – Glossary

AMD (Age-related macular degeneration) A disease occurring in people over 50 years of age that affects the macula of the eye and leads to progressive loss of central vision.

Advanced macular degeneration (advanced-stage or end-stage AMD) The late stage of AMD characterized by loss of central vision in one or both eyes.

AREDS (Age-Related Eye Disease Study) A study sponsored by the National Eye Institute which found that high doses of certain antioxidants and minerals could reduce the risk of developing advanced-stage AMD by roughly 25 percent.

AREDS 2 (Age-Related Eye Disease Study 2) A second and ongoing study aimed at determining the benefit of various AREDS formulations.

Amsler grid A grid of intersecting horizontal and vertical lines used to monitor central vision. A key tool in monitoring the progression of AMD.

Atrophic macular degeneration Dry AMD.

BCVA (best corrected visual acuity) Measure of the sharpest sight a person can achieve with corrective lenses.

Beta-carotene A compound of carotene found in dark green and dark yellow fruits and vegetables thought to be beneficial to eye health. May be contra-indicated in certain patients, such as current or previous smokers.

Bruch's membrane The innermost layer of the choroid, a layer of the eye that lies between the retina and the sclera, the outer protective layer or "white" of the eye.

Cataract A clouding of the lens of the eye or its surrounding membrane that obstructs the passage of light and leads to gradual vision loss.

Central vision The sharp, crisp vision in the center of our eyes for which the macula is responsible.

Choroid The vascular layer of the eye, also containing connective tissue, that lies between the retina and the sclera.

Choroidal neovascularization A type of wet AMD where abnormal blood vessels form under the macula and leak plasma and blood into it.

Cornea The transparent membrane in front of the iris and pupil that allows for the transmission of light.

Depth perception The aspect of vision having to do with the spatial relationship among different objects. The ability to judge distance.

Drusen Fatty protein deposits (usually in the form of yellow spots) that form beneath the retinal layer, thinning the macula and setting the stage for macular degeneration.

Dry AMD The most common form of AMD, characterized by slow but steady central vision loss due to degeneration of the macula.

Exudative macular degeneration Wet AMD.

Fellow eye The IMT patient's eye which has not received the implant.

Fluorescein angiography A technique for examining the circulation of the retina and choroid (the vascular layer of the eye that provides oxygen and nourishment to the outer layers of the retina), using intravenous dye and a specialized camera.

Intraocular telescope A tiny telescope surgically implanted in the eye which enlarges images up to three times in order that the macula can receive a broader picture across its more healthy regions restoring, to a point, the central vision lost due to AMD.

Lens A transparent structure within the eye that refracts light back to the retina.

Lutein A carotenoid found in the lens and macula of the eye that helps filter out damaging blue light.

LVR (Low Vision Rehabilitation) The process by which, through training and therapy, techniques are learned and skills developed in order to make the most of existing vision. LVR, while it does not restore sight, helps the patient maintain the highest possible quality of life with whatever vision capabilities still exist.

Macula The part of the retina responsible for sharp and accurate central vision. A healthy macula is vital to daily activities such as reading, driving, and even recognizing faces.

Ocular Relating to the eye. Resembling an eye in form or function.

Omega-3 fatty acids Found especially in fish oils, nuts, vegetable oils, and green leafy vegetables, this polyunsaturated fatty acid is characterized by three double bonds along the hydrocarbon chain. The omega-3 fatty acids DHA and EPA seem to play important roles in visual health.

Ophthalmology The branch of medical science dealing with the structure, function, and diseases of the eye.

Ophthalmologist A physician, a medical doctor trained in eye and vision care, capable of providing medical and surgical eyecare as well as eye exams.

Optometry The profession devoted to examining eyes, prescribing corrective measures, and diagnosing eye diseases.

Optometrist A professional (but not a physician) who provides eye exams, prescribes corrective lenses, provides low vision-aids and therapy, and diagnoses eye conditions like glaucoma, cataracts, and macular degeneration.

Optical coherence tomography The utilization of light waves to produce a high-resolution image of eye tissue.

Oxidation The chemical process by which potentially damaging (particularly to the eye) free radicals are released in the body.

Peripheral vision The outer part of the field of vision — what we call "side vision."

Retina The sensory membrane of the eye responsible for receiving images which have passed through the lens and converting those images into chemical and electrical signals which are dispatched to the brain via the optic nerve.

Retinal pigment epithelium A layer of dark-colored hexagonal cells next to the retina that nourishes the sight cells of the retina and removes waste products from them. It also shields the retina from excess incoming light.

Retina specialist An ophthalmologist who specializes in diseases associated with the retina and macula.

Subretinal neovascularization A type of wet AMD where abnormal blood vessels grow underneath the retina.

Supplements An ingestible product (vitamin or mineral) intended to supplement a diet or to meet dosage recommendations of certain vitamins or minerals.

Wet AMD AMD characterized by retinal bleeding or the growth of abnormal blood vessels beneath the macula. (Also called choroidalneovascularization; exudative macular degeneration, hemorrhagic macular degeneration, and subretinal neovascularization.)

Zeaxanthin An isomer of lutein found especially in fruits and vegetables. Zeaxanthin naturally concentrates in the macula helping to protect against damaging blue light and oxidation.

Appendix 2 – Resource Contact Information

I have always said, "Knowledge is power." In that spirit, I have listed here for you the resources I am familiar with that provide meaningful help to those fighting AMD. These include the names and contact information of: *foundations* raising money for research and education; *organizations* whose primary goal is to offer assistive care to low vision patients; *corporations* selling products meant to assist those dealing with low vision; *governmental agencies* that provide benefits, financial and otherwise; and *publications* I have found useful in obtaining more information about living with AMD.

These listings do not in any way represent an endorsement of any particular entity. Please take advantage of internet resources such as charitynavigator.org before you decide to donate money to any of the foundations or organizations listed on the following pages.

Hospitals and Universities Specializing in AMD Treatment and Research

This list includes some of the prominent names in the fight against AMD, listed alphabetically. To find a facility near you, ask your ophthalmologist or other health care professional.

Barnes Jewish Hospital
St. Louis, MO
314-747-3000
http://www.barnesjewish.org/

Bascom Palmer Eye Institute/University of Miami
Miami, FL
305-243-2020 / 888-845-0002
http://bascompalmer.org/

Cleveland Clinic Cole Eye Institute
Cleveland, OH
216-444-2020
http://my.clevelandclinic.org/eye/

Cullen Eye Institute/
Baylor College of Medicine/
Houston Methodist Hospital
Houston, TX
713-790-3333
http://www.houstonmethodist.org/

Doheny Eye Institute
Los Angeles, CA
323-442-7100
http://www.doheny.org/

Duke Eye Center

Durham, NC

919-684-6611

http://eyecenter.dukemedicine.org/eye_center/

Emory Eye Center

Atlanta, GA

404-778-2020

http://www.eyecenter.emory.edu/

Jules Stein Eye Institute

Los Angeles, CA

310-825-5000

http://jsei.org/

Keck School of Medicine / USC Eye Institute

Los Angeles, CA

800-872-2273

http://eye.keckmedicine.org

Kellogg Eye Center, University of Michigan

Ann Arbor, MI

734-763-8122

http://www.kellogg.umich.edu/

Massachusetts Eye & Ear Infirmary

Boston, MA

617-573-3202

http://www.masseyeandear.org/

The LuEsther T. Mertz Retinal Research Ctr. (Research)

New York, NY

http://retinal-research.org/about-retinal-research

Mayo Clinic

Rochester, MN

480-515-6296 / 480-342-2000

http://www.mayoclinic.org/departments-centers/ophthalmology

Moran Eye Center / University of Utah

Salt Lake City, UT

801-581-2352 / 877-248-6374

http://healthcare.utah.edu/moran/

New York Eye and Ear Infirmary of Mt. Sinai

New York, NY

212-979-4000

https://www.nyee.edu/

Retinal Consultants of Arizona

Phoenix, AZ

602-222-2221

http://www.retinalconsultantsaz.net/

UC Davis, University of California (Research)
Davis, CA
http://www.ucdavis.edu/

University of Iowa Hospitals and Clinics
Iowa City, IA
319-384-7222
http://www.uihealthcare.org/

Wills Eye Hospital
Philadelphia, PA
877-289-4557
https://www.willseye.org/

Wilmer Eye Institute at Johns Hopkins
Baltimore, MD
410-955-5080 / 800-215-6467
http://www.hopkinsmedicine.org/wilmer/

Government Agencies

Internal Revenue Service
800-829-1040

www.irs.gov

(Visually impaired people are eligible to receive certain tax benefits. They can deduct work-related expenses, certain unreimbursed medical expenses, and guide dog expenses. The legally blind can also take advantage of a higher standard deduction.)

Medicare / Medicaid
800-633-4227

www.cms.hhs.gov

National Eye Institute
301-451-2020

www.nei.nih.gov

(Blindness and low vision rehabilitation)

National Institute for Health
www.nih.gov

United States Department of Veterans Affairs
877-222-8387

www.va.gov/blindrehab

(Low vision benefits)

Foundations

AMD Alliance International

www.amdalliance.org

American Council for the Blind

800-424-8666

www.acb.org

American Foundation for the Blind

800-232-5463

www.afb.org

American Macular Degeneration Foundation

888-622-8527

www.macular.org

Associated Services for the Blind and Visually Impaired

215-627-0600

www.asb.org

Association for Macular Diseases

212-605-3719

www.macula.org

BrightFocus

800-437-2423

www.brightfocus.org

Columbia Lighthouse for the Blind

301-589-0894

www.clb.org

Foundation Fighting Blindness

800-683-5555

www.blindness.org

Lighthouse International

800-829-0500

www.lighthouse.org

Lions Clubs International

630-571-5466

www.lionsclubs.org

Macular Degeneration Partnership

310-623-4466

www.amd.org

Macula Foundation

800-622-8524

www.maculafoundation.org

National Council of State Agencies for the Blind

717-783-3784

www.ncsab.org

National Federation of the Blind

410-659-9314

www.nfb.org

Corporations

Amazon.com

www.amazon.com

(Books and a wide variety of other helpful products)

Amigo

800-692-6446

www.myamigo.com

(Scooters and powered chairs)

Bausch + Lomb

800-553-5340

www.bausch.com

(Eyeglasses, contact lenses, eye vitamins)

Hoveround

800-542-7236

www.hoveround.com

(Scooters and powered wheelchairs)

Independent Living Aids

800-537-2118

www.independentliving.com

(low vision aids, assistive technology)

LS&S ("Learning, Sight, and Sound Made Easier")

800-468-4789

www.lssproducts.com

(CCTV's, low vision lighting, talking products)

MaxiAids

800-522-6294

www.maxiaids.com

(CCTV's, low vision products, talking products)

Optelec

800-826-4200

us.optelec.com

(Text to speech readers, magnification products)

Appendix 3 – Recommended Reading

Duffy, Maureen A., and Irving R. Dickman.
Making Life more Liveable: Simple Adaptations for Living at Home after Vision Loss.
New York, NY: American Foundation for the Blind, 2002.

Mogk, Lylas G. M. D., and Marja Mogk, PhD.
Macular Degeneration: The Complete Guide to Saving and Maximizing Your Sight.
New York, NY: Random House Publishing Group, 2010.

Roberts, Daniel L.
The First Year: Age-Related Macular Degeneration: An Essential Guide for the Newly Diagnosed.
Cambridge, MA: De Capo Press, 2006.

Wolfe, Peggy R.
Macular Disease: Practical Strategies for Living with Vision Loss,
Second Edition. Minneapolis, MN: Park Publishing, 2011.

Bibliography

Bansal, Alok S., Paul Baker, and Julia A. Haller.
"An implantable visual prosthetic for end-stage macular degeneration,"
Expert Review Ophthalmology
6.2 (2011): 141-145.

Jager, Rama D., William F. Mieler, and Joan W. Miller.
"Age-related macular degeneration medical progress."
The New England Journal of Medicine
358.24 (June 12, 2008): 2606-2617.

Lim, Laurence S., Paul Mitchell, M. Johanna,
G. Frank, and Tien Y Wong.
"Ophthalmology 1: Age-related macular degeneration."
The Lancet
379.9827 (May 5 – May 11, 2012): 1728-1738.

Mogk, Lylas G., and Marja Mogk.
Macular Degeneration.
New York, NY: Random House Publishing Group, 2010.

Primo, Susan A.
"Implantable miniature telescope: Lessons learned."
Optometry – Journal of the American Optometric Association
81, no. 2 (Feb. 2010): 86-93.

Qiu, Qunghua, Yuan Yao, Zingwei Wu, and Dongmei Han.
"Higher dose lutein and a longer supplementation
period would be good for visual performance."
Nutrition 29.7/8 (July 2013): 1072.

Ratnapriya, R., and EY Chew.
"Age-related macular degeneration –
clinical review and genetics update."
Clinical Genetics
84, no. 2 (July 9, 2013): 160-166.

Scheiman, Mitchell, Maxine Scheiman,
and Stephen G. Whittaker.
*Low Vision Rehabilitation: A Practical Guide for
Occupational Therapists.*
Thorofare, NJ: SLACK, 2007.

Shikder, Shariful, Monjur Mourshed, and Andrew Price.
"Therapeutic lighting design for the elderly: a review."
Perspective in Public Health
132.6 (Nov 2012): 282-291.

Weir, Erica.
"Age-related macular degeneration: armed against AMD."
Canadian Medical Association Journal
170.4 (Feb. 17, 2004): 463-464.

Wolfe, Peggy R.
Macular Disease: Practical Strategies for Living with Vision Loss,
Second Edition. Minneapolis, MN: Park Publishing, 2011.

Acknowledgements

It is impossible to put into words the appreciation I have for the ophthalmology teams of Wilmer Eye Institute at Johns Hopkins, Baltimore, Maryland, and Wills Eye Hospital of Philadelphia, Pennsylvania. It is with great humility and gratitude that I express my heartfelt thanks to:

Morton Goldberg, M.D., Professor of Ophthalmology, and former Director of the Wilmer Eye Institute at Johns Hopkins

Oliver Schein, M.D., Professor of Ophthalmology

Judith Goldstein, O.D., F.A.A.O., Director of Low Vision Services at Wilmer Eye Institute; Assistant Professor of Ophthalmology

Tiffany Lauren Chan, Instructor of Ophthalmology

Katherine Cleveland, OTR/L, CLVT — occupational therapist

Dr. Julia Haller, M.D., Ophthalmologist-in-Chief at Wills Eye Hospital

I would like to acknowledge here also a number of other important people who have contributed a great deal to my life and this project:

My wife of fifty-six years, **Dixie**, and my **children** and **grandchildren**, all of whom have supported my efforts to accomplish things throughout my life. They have given me the emotional support and freedom to work on causes that mattered to me, from health care to Jiffy Lube to age-related macular degeneration.

My grandparents, **Mary** and **Thomas Wharton**, two strong foundation stones of my pyramid of success.

The team that worked closely with me through the many years of getting this book together — **Jan Oman**, **Darlene Sartain**, **Patrick Dempsey**, **Cindy Tracey**, and many others who contributed along the way. These people have been a tremendous assist to me throughout my endeavors, and the contributions they continue to make by way of support services of every kind, and friendship, are more and more essential to my life and work.

George Lois, Carol Cartaino, Patty Kyrlach, and **Roberta Greene,** who helped to see that the later stages of this book effort were brought to a professional and effective conclusion.

My advisory board: **John Sasser, Bruz Frenkil, Kay Freas,** and **Pam Felton,** who provided input every step of the way, and patiently put up with the drawn-out completion of this project.

A big thank-you, too, to the **Lions** of the world and to **Lions Clubs International** as well as the humanitarian arm of the Lions, the **Lions Clubs International Foundation.** Special thanks to Past International Director **Joseph F. Gaffigan** of Silver Spring, Maryland, for bringing the Hindman Foundation and the Lions army together in this monumental battle against age-related macular degeneration. The key to this relationship came from long-time friend and business associate **Bob Bullock.**

My many inspiring and helpful business associates, particularly in Jiffy Lube, the linchpin of my career.

All of the great teachers and coaches I was fortunate enough to have — too numerous to all be mentioned here, but all securely enshrined in my mind and memory.

Others in my early life who had a positive influence on me, from **Blind Bill** to the man who urged me to stand and fight for my rights when I was a young street kid.

The women caretakers at the various care facilities I spent time in, especially **Fern Crombie,** my house mother for many years at the Boys and Girls Home.

Donnie Black, **Vince Arioso**, and **Carlton Tronvold**, my three partners who went through school with me and then on to many other ventures and adventures together.

The great schools that were so important to my development as a person and member of society, from the public schools of Sioux City to Morningside College, The University of Minnesota and Harvard University.

The Masters in Hospital Administration program at the University of Minnesota, **James A. Hamilton**, Director, and **Marty Marshall**, head of the Owner/President Management Program at the Harvard Business School.

The **coaches**, **players**, and **administrators** of the colleges and junior colleges where I coached football.

Glenn Reno, my preceptor and mentor through my healthcare career and early Jiffy Lube years.

Don Schaefer, the Mayor of Baltimore, Governor of Maryland and a career friend.

The tremendously dedicated people who worked with me at **Youth Services International**, especially **Hank Felton**, who did so much to help young people get on the right track.

Now, Age-Related Macular Degeneration victims under 75 years of age have the chance to say, "Was blind, but now I see."

In October 2014, coinciding with the publication of this book, VisionCare, the creators and producers of the Implantable Miniature Telescope, received notice from the FDA to allow lowering the required age of the revolutionary treatment of late or end-stage macular degeneration from 75, to 65 years of age!

The long, challenging, and expensive path to this greatly needed approval was achieved by the persistence of Allen W. Hill, the CEO of VisionCare Ophthalmic Technologies, and the passionate efforts of Jim Hindman.

With this great step forward, many more thousands of victims of macular degeneration will be able to find a way back through the darkness.